MORE FIT 4 THE KINGDOM

DEAR RON + JANA —

JUST WANTED TO THANK YOU
BOTH FOR YOUR CONTINUAL
FRIENDSHIP, SUPPORT, +
ENCOURAGEMENT. HOPE YOU
ENJOY THIS BOOK + THE
PRINCIPALS BRING YOU
STRENGTH + HAPPINESS.

YOUR FRIEND,

MORE
FIT4THE
KINGDOM

Gain the spiritual strength the Savior emphasized
by following the training program He utilized

SKYE FAGRELL

To my wife, Jacque:

*For always loving, inspiring, and encouraging me to get this done.
This book, like all the other good things in our life,
wouldn't be possible without you.*

To my children, Alexa, Makenna, Gunner, and Jayda:

*For always making me so proud to be your dad,
for helping our family stick together,
and for laughing at my jokes!*

CONTENTS

Introduction
THE RACE OF LIFE

Lindsey Jacobellis was the favorite entering the event. The 20-year-old American and reigning World Champ had comfortably navigated her way into the women's medal round. Her event, the snowboard cross, was making its Olympic debut during the 2006 Turin games. As expected, she was dominating.

Snowboard cross follows a simple format; get down the course as quickly as possible. Described as "NASCAR on snow" due to its fast, congested, and difficult terrain, snowboard cross is a race to the finish. No points for style, just get down the course first and you win. Simple as that.

In the medal round, Lindsey raced out ahead of her three competitors. One crashed early on and another fell soon thereafter. As one of only two racers still on her feet, Lindsey was way out ahead as she approached the second to the last jump. The sport's most dominant and recognizable athlete was cruising to the finish, literally.

However, rather than going straight over the jump as she had in all the previous rounds, Lindsey pulled a showboat trick, a "method grab," in anticipation of her gold medal finish and in hopes of further exciting the crowd of exuberant fans. Yet, instead of the magazine cover finish she'd envisioned, she wiped out. Lindsey fell onto her back, and then spun off the course. She frantically managed to get back on her feet and headed toward the finish line, but it was too late. Desperately seeking to regain her momentum, Lindsey watched as Switzerland's Tanja Frieden raced past her for the gold.

To date, Lindsey has won 5 World Championships, 10 X Games Golds, and 29 World Cup Golds. She's easily the most decorated athlete in the history of snowboard cross. Yet, despite her great achievements, Lindsey's mistake lives on as a cautionary tale for racers worldwide.

The Race of Life

Like Lindsey, we're all involved in a race of sorts, the race of life. While our race shares many similarities with hers, there are a few fundamental differences. First, our race, or purpose, is to experience joy in this life and qualify for eternal life in the next (2 Ne. 2:25; Moses 1:39). There's no shortage of gold medals to distribute and Heavenly Father wants us all to succeed. Indeed, the earth was created, and the gospel was revealed so that families could be formed, sealed, and exalted eternally (Church, 2016). Second, in our race it really doesn't matter how fast we go, nor where we place in comparison to others. It's about the effort we're making to race according to the training we've received. Far more important than our pace, God is concerned about our direction and conduct along the way. Third, while crashes in races like the snowboard cross usually eliminate contestants from medal contention, in our race we can repeatedly crash and still find ourselves in contention for all the glory. It's not so much a matter of whether we'll crash or go off course - that's part of our racing experience. It's more about whether we'll choose to reach for the Savior's outstretched hand when we do (Matt. 14:29-31). To be clear, the cautionary tale about Lindsey isn't that she fell - it's that she let her guard down and it cost her an opportunity that she may never get back again.

Staying on Course

In order to stay on course, we need to be aware of the ever-increasing efforts to get us and our families off. We compete not only against difficult terrain, but against ferocious competitors bent on our destruction and focused on our failure. As these forces combine together, we must step up our efforts, or we'll succumb to theirs to bring us down (Eph. 6:12). Just as certain as it is that Heavenly Father wants us to have joy, and that the Savior has provided the way which we can, the adversary seeks that we all might become miserable like unto himself (2 Ne. 2:27). President Monson warned:

> "With his deceptions and lies, the adversary will lead you down a slippery slope to your destruction if you allow him to do so. You will likely be on that slippery slope before you even realize that there is no way to stop. You have heard the messages of the adversary. He cunningly calls: Just this once won't matter; everyone is doing it; don't be old-fashioned; times have changed; it can't hurt anyone; your life is yours to live" (Monson, 2015).

The righteous race of life, the strait and narrow path, is the only course that leads to happiness, joy, and peace (2 Nephi 31:20). The adversary knows this and will do all in his power to keep us from it. How vital it is that we exercise constant vigilance in order to avoid giving in to such lies and sliding off course, down his slippery slope.

In addition to being strait and narrow, the course we're on is somewhat like a treadmill, possessing not only the ability to increase in speed, but in incline, as well. All signs seem to indicate that both these variables will continue to intensify. Consequently, many Church leaders have been urging us to increase our personal and family spiritual fitness so that we can remain on it. To site just a few examples, let's start in October 2002, when we were told that the Church was going to "raise the bar" for missionary preparation and qualification. Elder Ballard introduced this change by comparing its urgency and necessity to war, stating:

> "We battle literally for the souls of men. The enemy is unforgiving and relentless. He is taking eternal prisoners at an alarming rate. And he shows no sign of letting up... While we are profoundly grateful for the many members of the Church who are doing great things in the battle for truth and right, I must honestly tell you it still is not enough. We need much more help... We don't need spiritually weak and semi-committed missionaries. We don't need you to just fill a position; we need your whole heart and soul" (Ballard, 2002).

A short time later, President Eyring added his witness. Speaking to the Church's seminary and institute teachers, he said:

"Too many of our students become spiritual casualties. Many go into the mission field and to the temple worthily. Yet your heart and mine aches when we think of a name and see a face of someone we taught and loved and then learned failed in the mission field or in a temple marriage... One such tragedy is too many. And yet the troubles and the temptations our students faced just five years ago pale in comparison with what we see now, and even more difficult times are ahead" (Eyring, 2003).

President Packer also invoked similar battle imagery and language when he declared:

"You are growing up in enemy territory. When you become mature spiritually, you will understand how the adversary has infiltrated the world around you. He is in homes, entertainment, the media, language— everything around you. In most cases, his presence is undetected... There are certain things that you must not do if the lines of communication are to remain open. You cannot lie or cheat or steal or act immorally and have those channels remain free from disruption. Do not go where the environment resists spiritual communication... You must learn to seek the power and direction that is available to you, and then follow that course no matter what" (Packer, 2012).

And not long ago, President Nelson acknowledged the increasing difficulty and dire nature of the battle we face when he said:

"...it will not be possible to survive spiritually without the guiding, directing, comforting, and constant influence of the Holy Ghost... My beloved brothers and sisters, I plead with you to increase your spiritual capacity..." (Nelson, 2018).

So how can we stay on our feet during this and future "perilous battles" and not get thrown off course? How can we keep our guard up and avoid the pitfalls that could cost us the "gold?" The answer is clear; become spiritually fit or, as the title of this book and the hymn *More Holiness Give Me* declares (Church, 2002, #131) – become "More Fit for the Kingdom!" I will outline later on why I've exchanged "for" for "4" in the title.

Surviving the Battle

The Stripling Warriors provide the template for the type of preparation that is needed. They gained the spiritual fitness needed to stay on course, and they gained it by making and keeping covenants. These 2000 young men (eventually 2060) promised to fight for liberty and to protect their lands, even if it meant they'd have to lay down their lives (Alma 53:16-17; Alma 57:8). Their strength is described in such terms as these:

- They were exceedingly valiant for courage, and also for strength and activity; but behold, this was not all—they were men who were true at all times in whatsoever thing they were entrusted (Alma 53:20)

- They were men of truth and soberness, for they had been taught to keep the commandments of God and to walk uprightly before him (Alma 53:21)

- They ... fought as if with the strength of God; ... and with such mighty power did they fall upon the Lamanites, that they did frighten them; and for this cause did the Lamanites deliver themselves up as prisoners of war (Alma 56:56)

While the difficult course being described is figurative, this is a spiritual reality. It's not a scare tactic. It's not a joke. It's not just good "bulletin board material." Using a sports analogy to emphasize the point, Elder Holland taught this truth frankly when he said:

"This is a life-and-death contest we are in... so I am going to get in your face a little, nose to nose, with just enough fire in my voice to singe your eyebrows a little—the way coaches do when the game is close, and victory means everything. And with the game on the line, what this coach is telling you is that to play in this match, some of you have to be more morally clean than you now are. In this battle between good and evil, you cannot play for the adversary whenever temptation comes along and then expect to suit up for the Savior at temple and mission time as if nothing has happened. That, my young friends, you cannot do. God will not be mocked.

"So, we need [individuals and families] already on the team to stay on it and stop dribbling out of bounds just when we need you to get in the game and play your hearts out! In almost all athletic contests of which I know, there are lines drawn on the floor or the field within which every participant must stay in order to compete. Well, the Lord has drawn lines of worthiness for those called to labor with Him in this work... You cannot travel down what Lehi called "forbidden paths" and expect to guide others to the 'strait and narrow' one—it can't be done" (Holland, 2011).

It's time to evaluate and to take action. As individuals and families, we must ask and answer questions such as, "How is my race going? Am I aware of the difficulties that lie ahead? Am I obtaining the training and spiritual fitness required?" In short, we need to ask ourselves, "Where do I stand?"

Raising the Bar for All Members

While some of the quotes used thus far have were directed toward youth in their original context, make no mistake; this instruction is applicable to all of us. In the same talk in which Elder Ballard "raised the bar" for missionary service, he also said to parents:

> "… if we are 'raising the bar' for your sons to serve as missionaries, that means we are also 'raising the bar' for you. If we expect more of them, that means we expect more of you and your wife as well. Remember, Helaman's 2,000 Stripling Warriors were faithful because 'they had been taught to keep the commandments of God and to walk uprightly before him' (Alma 53:21)—and that instruction came in their homes" (Ballard, 2002).

While becoming more spiritually fit is clearly the directive, how to do that is less defined. What "more fit" means for one individual or family might be something different for another. It could mean showing more love and kindness, or becoming more morally clean, or more capable to withstand the temptation to gossip, or a million other things. Regardless of the variety of weaknesses we may possess, the Lord stands ready to reveal the "training plan" to all who truly want increased spiritual fitness:

> "And if men come unto me, I will show unto them their weakness. I give unto men weakness that they may be humble; and my grace is sufficient for all men that humble themselves before me; for if they humble themselves before me, and have faith in me, then will I make weak things become strong unto them" (Eth. 12:27).

Making Weak Things Strong

When we humbly and prayerfully approach the Lord for help, like a coach (or coaching staff) preparing for the big game, He has promised to bless us with both the strength and strategies to enable us to come off victorious (DC 10:5). He will guide us in formulating offensive and defensive strategies unique to our strengths and weaknesses. These strategies often come in the form of "plays," or actions and commandments to perform. Some of the plays we might feel impressed to employ as individuals and families will increase our testimonies and strengthen our resolve. These include plays like prayer, scripture study, making the sabbath day a delight, church and temple attendance, or studying the teachings of latter-day prophets. Elder Stevenson pointed out that other plays might help prepare us for challenges yet to come, like thinking through scenarios and situations that might come our way and how to face them when we do (Stevenson, 2019). Finally, other plays might be more corrective in nature, devised to help get us back on track or to repent and repair of covenants and counsel we've neglected.

APPLICATION & DISCUSSION | INTRO | 1.0
Consider "Where You Stand" by answering the following:

1. *"What strategies and game plans need to be implemented?"* Consider the course you and your family are on. What strategies need to be employed?

   - Something to start: _____
   - Something to stop: _____
   - Something to continue: _____

2. *"What difficulties lie ahead?"* What challenges do you foresee coming? Consider the challenging and/or tempting scenarios that may come your way and what plan of action you'll take when they do?

   _____
   _____
   _____
   _____

3. *"Am I receiving the training and spiritual fitness required?"* How engaged have you and your family been in spiritual fitness? Consider your training and involvement in exercises like scripture reading, prayer, church attendance, etc. Are you hitting the spiritual gym on a regular basis? Are you listening to the coaches – Prophets, Parents, Church Leaders?

   _____
   _____
   _____
   _____

(For a blank copy of this "Application & Discussion" see the Appendix)

In any case, the Lord taught that those who are faithful and diligent will be, "...crowned with blessings from above, yea, and with commandments not a few, and with revelations in their time..." (D&C 59:4). Just as people desiring increased physical fitness understand it will only come at the cost of increased physical activity and discipline, individuals and families seeking spiritual fitness shouldn't be surprised that "more" will be required. Initially, this can seem discouraging, but the Lord's purpose in "increasing the load" or changing our "routine" is benevolent, not burdensome. President Monson taught this plainly:

> "God's commandments are not given to frustrate us or to become obstacles to our happiness. Just the opposite is true. He who created us and who loves us perfectly knows just how we need to live our lives in order to obtain the greatest happiness possible. He has provided us with guidelines which, if we follow them, will see us safely through this often treacherous mortal journey" (Monson, 2015. See also D&C 82:8-10).

This concept, known in the fitness world as "The Overload Principle," will be discussed in greater detail in chapter 4 of this book.

Becoming & Remaining Strong

Regardless of the specific weakness we need strengthened, the time to *become* and *remain* strong is now! The strength we had in the past, and what we did to gain it, won't be enough to successfully navigate the future. Unlike Lindsey Jacobellis, we can't let our guard down. Like the Stripling Warriors, we need to make and keep covenants and learn to obey with exactness (Alma 57:21). This will require adjustments throughout our race, but that's how improvement is made; looking for small changes we can make in things we do often.

How do we gain the type of spiritual strength required? How do we steadily develop the necessary level of spiritual fitness to survive the conflict of our time? President Ezra Taft Benson gave the answer nearly 60 years ago when, as an Apostle, he taught:

> "It seems to me that the most successful program of complete youth fitness ever known to man was described in fourteen words: 'And Jesus increased in wisdom and stature and in favor with God and man.' There is the ideal of any program of youth fitness, to help our youth increase in wisdom and stature and in favor with God and man" (Benson, 1960. See also Luke 2:52).

This is the reason why the title of this book is *"More Fit 4 the Kingdom"* and not simply *"More Fit for the Kingdom."* I've found in my church service as a Bishop that youth and adults who come to confess a spiritual ailment and focus their improvement only on that one issue are far less likely to overcome their weakness than those who focus on their total wellness and overall fitness in the four areas outlined by President Benson and Luke. For example, like most Bishops, I've met with numerous individuals who've struggled with pornography. My experience has been that individuals who work only on strengthening and overcoming that weakness can have success, but not near as much as those who simultaneously seek to increase their fitness in the other areas modeled by the Savior. The most successful individuals I've worked with have identified and set goals to improve not only spiritually, but intellectually, physically, and socially, as well. When individuals and families who are struggling with a spiritual ailment start accomplishing goals in all of the other areas of fitness (which are often more easily measurable than the spiritual one they initially sought my assistance for) they become increasingly motivated to continue the process of repentance. Thus, throughout this book when I refer to the process of becoming more fit, I'll do so as, "More Fit 4 Life." This serves as an intentional and deliberate reminder of the importance of a balanced approach to growth in all four areas of fitness.

Applying True Principles

There are at least a few reasons why increasing fitness levels in other areas of fitness assist in the spiritual area people may initially be struggling with. First, a basic premise of this book is that true principles apply in a wide variety of circumstances (Scott, 1993). For example, while most feel that gaining physical strength is challenging, they have no problem with the idea of planning, tracking, and measuring their efforts to attain it. Yet when asked to plan, track, and measure their intellectual, spiritual, or social efforts, most are skeptical that such an approach is applicable to such "unquantifiable" pursuits. They are especially skeptical in regard to their spiritual improvement efforts. Unfortunately, this is a major misconception and one of the main reasons so many people become stagnant in their overall development. Tony Horton, creator of the popular P90X workout program, said it this way:

> "There's no doubt that taking care of yourself physically can help you with almost any purpose.

When you feel better, you accomplish more – and that's not just some motto I got from a bumper sticker. A recent study out of Brigham Young University shows that people with poor diets suffered a 66 percent loss of workplace productivity. The numbers don't lie: Taking care of yourself enables you to be more productive – and that means you'll get more out of life" (Horton, 2014).

Simply put, if a principle works in the weight room to stimulate muscle growth and strength, it also works in the family room to stimulate spiritual growth and strength. By extension, it will also work in our intellectual and social arenas.

Second, a repentant sinner (an individual or family seeking spiritual improvement) gains confidence in the process of their spiritual development as they see it in their physical development. It's much like the lesson Alma taught the Zoramites. Using a physical example to teach a spiritual concept, Alma compared a seed to the process of strengthening faith:

"...if you give place, that a seed may be planted in your heart, behold, if it be a true seed, or a good seed... it will begin to swell within your breasts; and when you feel these swelling motions, ye will begin to say within yourselves – it must needs be that this is a good seed, or that the word is good... And now, behold, will not this strengthen your faith? Yea, it will strengthen your faith: for ye will say I know that this is a good seed; for behold it sprouteth and beginneth to grow" (Alma 32:28,30).

Seeing the fruits of their labors in a physical way, the seeker of spiritual improvement is inclined to continue applying the same principle in their spiritual life. The motivation of weight loss, increased strength, and improved physical appearance drives their enthusiasm to continue their spiritual exercises, not only aiding them in their efforts to gain a new shape, but to become a "new creature" in Christ (Mosiah 27:24-26).

Third, the individual or family seeking spiritual improvement eventually no longer needs to look anywhere else for evidence that the spiritual process they are engaged in will bring forth good fruit. Having walked the path, held the rod, and managed their way through the mists of darkness, they've partaken of the fruit for themselves. They've discovered that the fruit at the end of the covenant path is "sweet" above all that they have ever tasted and want its joy and happiness for themselves and others (1 Nephi 8:10-12). As a result of their reliance on the teachings and atonement of Jesus Christ, they feel the explosive power of God's redeeming love, His grace both compelling and enabling them to change (Alma 5:9-14).

Thus, our efforts at improvement in any one area of fitness are enhanced as we focus on improvement in all four areas of fitness. In short, our efforts become more effective because we can see and feel that "it's working!" No wonder this pattern is the basis for the new primary and youth initiative of the Church: "The initiative is to focus on setting and achieving goals for spiritual, social, physical, and intellectual development…" (Church, 2018).

Becoming More Fit 4 the Kingdom

This is the answer to the question posed earlier, *"How* do I become more spiritually fit?" Simply put, we follow the Savior. We gain the spiritual strength the Savior *emphasized* by following the training program the Savior *utilized*. That is the purpose of this book - to outline how fundamental, time-tested, and proven principles of physical fitness also apply in gaining spiritual strength and power. While these same principles also aid in gaining increased fitness in the intellectual and social arenas of our lives - and some attention and examples will be given there - the primary focus of this book will be on utilizing physical examples to make spiritual applications.

Like physical strength, spiritual fitness comes only at the price of dedication, perseverance, and self-discipline. Just as increased physical fitness enables us to accomplish feats we were once incapable of, these same principles will enable us to gain the spiritual strength necessary to stand strong in the face of the same temptations that once took us down. Like the Stripling Warriors (Alma 57:25-26), we can gain the spiritual strength necessary to become invincible!

3. More purity give me,
More strength to o'ercome,
More freedom from earth-stains,
More longing for home.
More fit for the kingdom,
More used would I be,
More blessed and holy —
More, Savior, like thee.
(Church, 2002, #131)

THE RACE OF LIFE | *core concepts*

- Remember, the reason for including the story about Lindsey Jacobellis isn't that she fell. It's that she let her guard down and it cost her an opportunity that she may never get back again.

- In addition to being "strait and narrow," the course we're on is somewhat like a treadmill, possessing not only the ability to increase in speed, but in incline, as well. All signs seem to indicate that both these variables will continue to intensify.

- The Stripling Warriors provide the template for the type of preparation that is needed. They gained the spiritual fitness needed to stay on course, and they gained it by making and keeping covenants.

- Regardless of what specific weakness we or our families need strengthened, the time to become and remain strong is now! The strength we had in the past, and what we did to gain it, won't be enough to successfully navigate the future.

- The most successful program of complete youth fitness ever known to man was described in fourteen words: "And Jesus increased in wisdom and stature and in favor with God and man."

- If a principle works in the weight room to stimulate muscle growth and strength, it will also work in the living room to stimulate spiritual growth and strength.

- Our efforts at improvement in any one area of fitness is enhanced as we focus on improvement in all areas of fitness: intellectual, physical, spiritual, and social.

- We gain the spiritual strength the Savior *emphasized* by following the training program the Savior *utilized*.

Chapter 1
CHOOSING TO CHANGE

Choosing to change started early for Eldrick. As the legend goes, he was only 10 months old when he climbed down from his highchair, grabbed a plastic toy golf club, and began mimicking his father Earl's left-handed swing. After a couple of weeks of swinging, he apparently grew dissatisfied with his motion. As his father looked on, Eldrick changed to the other side of the ball, switched his hands, found the proper right-handed grip, and began practicing all over again. Earl called to his wife: "We have a genius on our hands!" (Eden, 2013).

The "genius" Earl was referring to was his son's amazing natural ability and athleticism. But Eldrick's willingness, courage, and ability to change is genius, as well. Switching from golfing left-handed to right-handed isn't the only change Eldrick has made over the years. He's changed his name, as well. In fact, most don't know him by Eldrick anymore at all. He simply goes by "Tiger" now.

Having been the best or among the best golfers in the world most of the last 20+ years hasn't seduced Eldrick "Tiger" Woods into becoming content with his game. Not only has he continually made subtle tweaks, but he's chosen to completely disassemble and reconstruct his swing multiple times. To many experts, this was unnecessary risk taking, and they could point out numerous golfers whose attempt at change turned out to be disastrous. But for Tiger, they were necessary steps in his progress as a competitor and to compensate for changes in his body due to age and injury. The result? 15 majors and 81 wins... and counting!

In Order to Change We Must Make an Exchange!

Progression from one point to another – whether it's intellectual, physical, spiritual, or social – comes only at the cost of change. Additionally, that change only comes as the result of an exchange we make in our lives. Someone hoping to lose weight may choose to exchange their daily 40 oz. soda habit for ice water. A family wanting to draw closer together and to God may choose to exchange a few hours of television time and Instagram scrolling for time at the Temple together or working on Family History. The examples could go on in every area of fitness, but the principle is clear and can be summed up with an old Texas adage: "If all you ever do is all you've ever done, then all you'll ever get is all you ever got."

The process of making an exchange (when we trade in one habit or condition for another) in order to make progress (so we can move from one station to another) is taught in one of the few scriptural references we have in regard to the Savior's development. The scriptures teach that "he received not a fulness at first but received grace *for* grace; and he received not a fulness at first, but continued grace *to* grace, until he received a fulness" (DC 93:12-13, emphasis added). Note the difference in the "grace phrases." The phrase "grace *for* grace" implies the exchange. The phrase "grace *to* grace" implies the progression. While we're left to ponder what exchanges the Savior may have made as he grew in "wisdom and stature, and in favor with God and man" (Luke 2:52), it's both comforting and encouraging to know that the process is the same for all of us. As previously stated, if we follow the program the Savior utilized, we'll gain the strength He emphasized.

Thus, in order to change – to progress from our current spiritual condition closer *to* the condition He's at - we must make an exchange! Spiritually speaking, that exchange is always our will *for* His. The scriptures teach, "For if you keep my commandments you shall receive of his fulness, and be glorified in me as I am in the Father; therefore, I say unto you, you shall receive grace for grace" (DC 93:20). We read further, "He that keepeth his commandments receiveth truth and light, until he is glorified in truth and knoweth all things" (DC 93:28). Knowing how favorable the "exchange rate" is, it's surprising how difficult it often is for us to choose to trade our will in!

Of course, this process works in both directions. In the physical realm, when someone temporarily experiences a disabling circumstance, like a broken arm, their muscles "atrophy." This means their muscles literally start to weaken, decrease in size, and waste away. Alarmingly, a muscle in disuse can experience atrophy in as little as two weeks! This same phenomenon can happen spiritually as well. As we willingly choose to exchange righteous/productive habits for wicked/slothful ones, our spiritual strength weakness and wastes away. This diminishing process is stated bluntly in the scriptures: "And they that will harden their hearts, to them is given the lesser portion of the word until they know nothing concerning his mysteries…" (Alma 12:11).

When We're Through Changing - We're Through

Change is essential for growth and development, both as an athlete and as a disciple. Elder Packer stated powerfully, "Things that don't change remain the same… And when we are through changing – we're through" (Robbins, 2018). Whether on a golf course like Tiger Woods, or in the classroom, workplace, family, or our relationship with God, our ability to maximize performance and productivity depends on our ability to change in positive ways.

Anyone who has ever tried to change knows it's far from easy. Change can be slow and frustrating, monotonous and painful. Ironically, it can also be the most rewarding thing we will ever do (Mosiah 27:24-29). The concept of changing is closely related to repenting. Essentially, repentance means "striving to change" or "steady improvement." Just like some athletes can be reluctant to change, the call to repent (to become more spiritually fit) is often met with reluctance, as well. Elder Christofferson explained:

> "When prophets come crying repentance [or change], it 'throws cold water on the party.' But in reality, the prophetic call should be received with joy. Without repentance [or change], there is no real progress or improvement in life." (Christofferson, 2011; "change" added for emphasis)

To repent - to change and improve - "is [the Gospel's] most frequent message," taught Elder Oaks. "Repenting [changing and improving] means giving up all of our practices—personal, family, ethnic, and national—that are contrary to the commandments of God. The purpose of the gospel is to transform common creatures into celestial citizens, and that requires change" (Oaks, 2003). No question about it; the gospel of Jesus Christ challenges us to change. With so much upside, with so much encouragement from intellectual, physical, spiritual, and social experts, why is change so hard for us to embrace?

APPLICATION & DISCUSSION | CH 1 | 1.0

Consider and share how repentance - change and improvement - has strengthened you:

1. *What is an area that you or your family have already worked at and been successful in improving?*

   _____

   _____

   _____

   _____

2. *How might life be different had that change not been made?*

   _____

   _____

   _____

   _____

(For a blank copy of this "Application & Discussion" see the Appendix)

Denying & Delaying Change

One of the reasons for our reluctance toward repentance is the relentless reminders from the adversary that we *can't* change. Sure, it's an obvious lie, but many accept it. We all bring good traits, habits, and characteristics from childhood into adolescence and then adulthood, but we also all bring some "not-so-good things," or "baggage." This baggage often causes us to think, feel, and behave as we were in the past, rather than the different person we are or who we are striving to become. I've seen this over the years in my profession as a seminary teacher. Early on in my career, I read and adopted President Packer's philosophy of welcoming new missionaries to the field when he was a Mission President. It goes as follows:

> "I assume that you are mature. I look upon you as being old enough to be able to learn and sensible enough to want to. Right now, I may not know who you really are or where you have been or what you have done. Most of that, depending on you, will not matter. I take you just as you are and stamp you 'A-Grade, Number 1.' You can prove yourself to be less than that, but you will have to work at it. I will be very reluctant to believe it. If there is something about yourself that you do not like, now is the time to change it. If there is something in your past that has been disabling, spiritually or otherwise, now is the time to rise above it" (Packer, 1977).

While in most cases I've found students have responded very positively to this and have happily dropped the weighty baggage of their pasts, others have really struggled. They've seemed bent on sabotaging their own progress or perception in the eyes of others, holding on to old baggage as though it's some sort of validation that they are "unique" or "experienced." Unfortunately, this baggage and our reluctance to let go of it is often the evidence the adversary uses to discourage and persuade us to believe we're stuck as we are. This "baggage issue" weighs down families in the same way.

The Bucket of Crabs

On a related note, I've seen other students in seminary and in youth classes at Church who are eager to let go of their past but are prevented because of their peers. This sad scenario is often referred to as the "bucket of crabs" syndrome. Some of these "crabs" reach up and pull others down due to their lack of forgiveness or belief that people really can change. Perhaps they feel threatened or question the sincerity of those trying to change. Whatever the cause, these crabs deny the Savior's atoning power to those seeking to secure it and are themselves in sore need of repentance. To these I share the Savior's admonition:

> "Wherefore, I say unto you, ye ought to forgive one another; for he that forgiveth not his brother his trespasses standeth condemned before the Lord; for there remaineth in him the greater sin. I, the Lord, will forgive whom I will forgive, but of you it is required to forgive all men" (D&C 64:9-10).

Other crabs operate from a different sort of motivation. Unlike the previous example, these peers couldn't care less whether their friend is worthy of the Savior's grace or is genuine in their desire to change. Their motivation to pull their friend down stems from their own selfishness and insecurities; they don't want to lose one of their "partners in crime." As they flail around, hoping to find happiness in wickedness, they want everyone else to be miserable like themselves (Alma 41:10, 2 Nephi 2:27).

In either case, those doing the pulling down whisper along with the adversary, *"You can't change. You won't change. It's too long and too hard to change."* Sadly, the struggle to break free often gives way to the tireless tugs and taunts of those deep within the bucket, or as Nephi calls it, "the great and spacious building" (1 Nephi 8:25-28). Once seeking a newness of life, these individuals (or families) now descend back into the bucket and find themselves even more convinced they can't change.

Self-Justification

Another branch of the "I *can't* change" philosophy is a slightly different lie. I'll call this the *"I shouldn't change because that's just the way I am"* lie. Elder Hallstrom shared a story of a person who had fallen victim to this deception. This man had a troubled relationship with his wife and was estranged from their children. He struggled to keep employment, had no close friends, and found interaction with ward members so difficult he finally was unwilling to serve in the Church. During one intense discussion about the challenges in his life, he leaned toward Elder Hallstrom—at the conclusion to their numerous talks—and said, "Bishop, I have a bad temper, and that's just the way I am!" (Hallstrom, 2014).

What's the motive for adopting this lie? Well, there are at least a couple of answers. One is self-justification. From Nephi we read:

> "And there shall also be many which shall say: Eat, drink, and be merry; nevertheless, fear God—he will justify in committing a little sin; yea, lie a little, take the advantage of one because of his words, dig a pit for thy neighbor; there is no harm in this; and do all these things, for tomorrow we die; and if it so be that we are guilty, God will beat us with a few stripes, and at last we shall be saved in the kingdom of God... and thus

the devil cheateth their souls, and leadeth them away carefully down to hell"(2 Nephi 28:8,21).

Elder Holland added similar sentiment when he said with great clarity, "Please spare me your speeches about 'That's just the way I am.' I've heard that from too many people who wanted to sin and call it psychology" (Holland, 2017). Enough said!

Our Favorite Sins

Additionally, our *"that's just the way I am"* leanings may also stem from some of our aforementioned baggage. The *"I've given up most of my past sins but still want to hang on to my favorites"* type of baggage. These "favorites" not only manifest themselves in the sinful behavior we try to justify, but in the form of ingrained habits, practices, or tendencies. As individuals and families, we may have found some level of success or happiness in the past, maybe not as much as we could have had, but it leads us to reason: "Why mess with it?!" Putting closeness to God in terms of food, we recognize that we aren't eating from the finest of restaurants or receiving the fullest of servings but rationalize that the crumbs and scraps we do receive aren't too bad.

Tiger Woods personifies the exact opposite of this "why mess with it" reasoning. In a *Time* magazine article, Dan Goodgame compared Tiger's relentless drive for excellence to what the Japanese call "kaizen," or continuous improvement. "Toyota engineers will push a perfectly good assembly line until it breaks down," wrote Goodgame. "Then they'll find and fix the flaw and push the system again. That's kaizen. That's Tiger" (Goodgame, 2000).

Most athletes are different than Tiger. They become so good at a bad technique that it becomes hard for them to break out of it. Their reluctance to change is compounded when they've not only grown comfortable with the bad technique but have had success with it as well. Fearing the short-term learning curve and potential lack of production that might accompany it, they sacrifice the long-term benefits and put off change entirely. What was once only a minor flaw that could have been easily fixed becomes a career-long "hole in their game."

Choose to Change!

Do any of these scenarios, questions, or rationalizations sound familiar to you? Whichever one be the case, Elder Hallstrom responded to such thinking by teaching:

> "...once any of us conclude — 'That's just the way I am,' we give up our ability to change. We might as well raise the white flag, put down our weapons, concede the battle, and just surrender — any prospect of winning is lost. While some of us may think that does not describe us, perhaps every one of us demonstrates by at least one or two bad habits, 'That's just the way I am'" (Hallstrom, 2014).

Here's the bottom line: the adversary doesn't care which lie we accept. It makes no difference to him because he wins, regardless. Our choice to postpone - or put off change entirely - meets the adversary's purpose. To be clear, his objective is to prevent us from receiving blessings, opportunities, spiritual guidance, and become "miserable like unto himself" (2 Ne. 2:27). So, while we all have baggage, we don't have to carry it with us! We can change, and we can choose to trust the Savior who said, "Come unto me, all ye that are burdened and heavy laden, and I will give you rest... For behold, I, God, have suffered these things for all, that they might not suffer if they would repent [or change]" (Matt. 11:28; DC 19:16).

True happiness can only be found by being washed clean through faith in Jesus Christ, by continuing repentance, and by making and keeping covenants. We know this, and Satan knows it, too. As a result, he does all he can to prevent our personal purification. Truly, "[one] of the most serious human defects in all ages is procrastination" (Kimball, 1982). Whether we're putting off the impression to eat better, exercise more, start a personal scripture study program, or talk to our Bishop, denying or delaying such feelings will cause us to become further entangled in the undesirable behavior. As a result, finding our way back to the gym - or to closeness with God – becomes even more difficult to do.

APPLICATION & DISCUSSION | CH 1 | 1.1

Carefully evaluate whether you or your family have accepted the *"I can't change"* or *"I shouldn't change"* philosophy in any of the four areas of fitness. Are there areas in which you've concluded, *"That's just the way I am"* or *"That's just the way we are."*

1. Wisdom – *In your intellectual fitness efforts?*

_____

_____

_____

2. Stature – *In your physical fitness efforts?*

_____

_____

_____

3. In Favor with God – *In your spiritual fitness efforts?*

_____

_____

_____

4. In Favor with Man – *In your social fitness efforts?*

_____

_____

_____

(For a blank copy of this "Application & Discussion" see the Appendix)

Choosing the Path of Change

So, once we've seen through the lies about change and embraced that we can and should seek it, a choice must be made in regard to the direction we change course toward. This choice takes both great courage and faith. First, courage to acknowledge aspects of ourselves or our family life that we don't like and to begin charting a new course. The Lord described the courage needed to proceed with difficult changes like this when He taught, "Be strong and of a good courage; be not afraid, neither be thou dismayed: for the Lord thy God is with thee whithersoever thou goest." (Joshua 1:9) Second, we must have faith and a fundamental trust in the vision of who, what, and where we want to be in the future. We must have faith that our commitment to change will help create a new and better life. If we don't believe an exercise plan will help us gain strength, we aren't going to be motivated to follow it. Likewise, if we don't believe studying Come Follow Me will bring our family increased spiritual strength, we won't be very motivated to do it either. Thus, we must also have faith that good things will happen when that change is made. The Lord outlined the connection between faith, change, and strength saying:

"And if men come unto me I will show unto them their weakness. I give unto men weakness that they may be humble; and my grace is sufficient for all men that humble themselves before me; for if they humble themselves before me, and have faith in me, then will I make weak things become strong unto them" (Eth. 12:27).

The Cheshire Cat of Lewis Carroll's classic novel, Alice's Adventures in Wonderland, taught a profound truth about the direction we choose to change toward. In answering Alice's inquiry, "Which path shall I follow?" the Cat answered frankly, "That depends where you want to go. If you do not know where you want to go, it doesn't matter which path you take." When Alice informed the Cat that she didn't care where, he quickly and accurately confirmed, "Then it doesn't matter which way you go" (Carroll, 1898). With that, Alice set off, content not so much to arrive at a specified destination, but happy to get "somewhere."

The "Alice-like" Approach

Most of us believe ourselves to be quite unlike Alice. We've mustered the requisite courage and faith. We know where we want to go and what our goal is; to live eternally with our families, our Heavenly Parents, and our Savior. Further, we understand that the path we choose to follow in this life will lead to our destination in the next life. President Monson, who often employed the interaction of Alice and the Cheshire Cat in talks he delivered throughout his ministry, once said the following truth after recounting the tale:

"Unlike Alice, we all know where we want to go, and it does matter which way we go, for by choosing our path, we choose our destination... Decisions are constantly before us. To make them wisely, courage is needed—the courage to say no, the courage to say yes. Decisions do determine destiny... I plead with you to make a determination right here, right now, not to deviate from the path which will lead to our goal: eternal life with our Father in Heaven" (Monson, 2010).

Thus, knowing the importance of choices in reaching the desired destination, most of us are also quick to identify fundamental "exercises" that will strengthen us on our journey. Among these, many include a plan and exercises such as prayer, gospel study, sabbath day worship, and temple attendance. Much like the benefits of push-ups, pull-ups, sit-ups, and cardiovascular exercise, there isn't any question about the effectiveness of these spiritual exercises, nor of their importance in any plan to become More Fit 4 the Kingdom. However, the approach most of us often take to applying these fundamental exercises is much more "Alice-like" than we might realize.

The application of the principles that govern physical and spiritual fitness are inseparable. Optimal fitness in both areas, along with our development intellectually and socially, should be the goal of all. Elder Klebingat taught this truth directly:

"Your soul consists of your body and spirit (see D&C 88:15). Feeding the spirit while neglecting the body, which is a temple, usually leads to spiritual dissonance and lowered self-esteem. If you are out of shape, if you are uncomfortable in your own body and can do something about it, then do it! Elder Russell M. Nelson has taught that we should 'regard our body as a temple of our very own' and that we should 'control our diet and exercise for physical fitness'" (Klebingat, 2014).

The Spirit is Willing, but the Flesh is Weak

Application can also be found in Peter's oft-quoted response to the Savior in the garden of Gethsemane, "The spirit is indeed willing, but the flesh is weak" (Matt. 26:41). This statement was made when Peter, James, and John were found asleep after having been given the charge by the Savior to keep watch as he prayed. While Peter's challenge in staying awake was physical fatigue, many of us find ourselves in a similar plight; spiritually limited as a result of our physical well-being, or lack thereof. As mentioned in the introduction, while a focus on increased physical fitness is usually not considered when hoping to mend what's spiritually ailing us, the two are inseparable.

Let me illustrate an example of this relationship, by sharing a composite of multiple experiences I've had as Bishop. A couple in my ward, let's call them "John and Sally," set up an appointment to meet with me. They shared the struggles that they were having. They'd been going on for years. Their challenges were serious. Like most marriages, there were problems and like most problems in marriage, they both shared the blame. They didn't know what to do and were at a crossroads. They had been to professional marriage counseling already and were willing to continue. But they were frustrated with the lack of difference their efforts to change and improve their marriage had seemed to make. They were humbly seeking help from both professional and ecclesiastical leaders. While I knew I didn't know how to fix their problems, I was confident the Lord did. They wanted to save their marriage and were willing to work on it. Miracles happen when those factors combine.

Whenever I'm in situations like this, I try to help the couple identify aspects of the four areas of fitness they can strive to strengthen individually, outside of the obvious area they've come to see me about. So, in my mind I think, "Jesus grew in wisdom (intellectual/professional) and stature (physical), and in favor with God (spiritual) and man (social); how can I assist John and Sally in each area?" I then interview them and ask questions to help assess where they're at. My approach with John might then go something like this:

- Intellectually / Professionally = He's working hard and doing all he can to further his career and provide for his family.

- Physically = He's not happy with his fitness. The discouragement he feels from his marriage and stress from work have led to long lapses in exercise...

- Spiritually = Seems like John is making a genuine effort, but he needs more frequency and follow-up...

- Socially = He and Sally are meeting with a solid marriage counselor and are working hard to implement his instruction.

Going through a process like this enable the individual to identify strengths and weakness while also helping me identify where I can be of most help. Sometimes as a result of the interview, I feel impressed to get some mentors involved. If so, in a case like this, I'd let John know that I think mentors could be a great asset to him and ask his permission for me to reach out to some men that I feel could help. If he'd agree, I'd invite one to become a "spiritual mentor," and another to become his "physical mentor." I'd ask these men to contact John regularly, help him set some goals, offer training and support, and follow-up as frequently as possible. I've always been impressed with the inspired plans these mentors and "Johns and Sally's" come up with. In some cases, I've found individuals and their mentors selecting a church program like Preach My Gospel as a spiritual strength training program. In others, I've seen them going to the temple together on a monthly basis. Some just call daily and share a scripture together. Some mentors are out in the neighborhood, jogging with their mentee or meeting at the gym. I've learned that they're eating better, tracking their steps, or have adopted a "water consumption" goal together. The programs very as needs are adapted to individual, but the result is the same: They get stronger. They grow closer to the Lord. They grow closer as a couple. They gain lifelong friends in their mentors and expand the circle of people they can count on. Most importantly, they learn the goal setting techniques necessary to continue gaining the strength the Savior emphasized by following the program He utilized!

Many factors contribute to these results. Perhaps it's the boost that comes from setting and achieving goals in the various spiritual or physical plans they participate in. Maybe it's the sense of accomplishment in seeing and feeling the tangible changes made through diligent effort, such as closeness to the Spirit or increased physical energy. The possibilities could go on, but whatever the cause, the connection is clear; our spiritual fitness is aided by physical fitness.

The Flesh is Willing, but the Spirit is Weak

The opposite may also be the reason some fail to take action; "the *flesh* is indeed willing, but the *spirit* is weak." We can look to the mighty Samson for a perfect example of this inverse relationship (Judges 14-16). Samson, raised up to help free the Israelites who'd fallen captive as a result of their wickedness, could have become a powerful spiritual leader and helped his people forsake their sins. However, he fell extremely short of this potential, having "great physical strength but [being] weak in intellectual and moral character" (Church, Bible Dictionary, Samson). While it would be easy for us to read of the many stories describing Samson's superhuman strength and conclude that the Lord was with him, it is clear He was not.

Having made a Nazarite oath, which included both outward and inward commitments, Samson's failure to live up to it left him void of the power that comes from keeping covenants (D&C 82:10). While he kept one notable requirement associated with the oath – his long hair – he mistakenly placed his confidence in that single outward symbol, rather than in God and the far more important inward requirements of the oath (Numbers 6:2-7). When Delilah's treachery finally led to his hair being cut, there was no actual loss of physical strength. However, the action broke his misplaced confidence – ironically leading him to realize that not only had his hair been cut, but the final thread tying him to his already ineffective vows.

Like a young man with a missionary haircut and a white shirt may take confidence in knowing he "looks the part," Samson was trusting that his lone outward sign of righteousness would save him. Elder Holland taught accordingly:

"No missionary can be unrepentant of sexual transgression or profane language or pornographic indulgence and then expect to challenge others to repent of those very things! You can't do that. The Spirit will not be with you, and the words will choke in your throat as you speak them" (Holland, 2011).

Make no mistake about it; God was no more with Samson before his final haircut then He was after, nor was Samson's physical strength any greater before his haircut than it was after. If Samson was capable of bench-pressing 400 pounds prior to his haircut, he was capable of benching 400 pounds after. His weakness was a realization of his wickedness. When the outward symbol was destroyed, so was his confidence (DC 121:45-46; DC 63:16). Thus, he became miserable and broken; a man whose flesh was willing, but his spirit too weak to lead him into action.

Summary

Learning that our spirit and our body are combined in such a way that "our body becomes an instrument of our mind and the foundation of our character" (Packer, 2003) many individuals and families conclude that they should eat healthier and try to get in better physical condition. This is wise. The goal or "destination" which they hope to obtain or arrive at is "Physical Fitness." They may also loosely identify the plan or "way" to get there; diet and exercise. Now, while this is definitely a good start to getting to the desired destination, there are still quite a few things to consider. Elder Ballard taught:

"Some have difficulty differentiating between a goal and a plan until they learn that a goal is a destination or an end, while a plan is the route by which you get there... Goal setting is essentially beginning with the end in mind. And planning is devising a way to get to that end" (Ballard, 2007).

Some of the potential variables a person hoping to become more physically fit might consider, are questions such these:

1. *What kind of "better shape" do I want; lean out or more mass?*
2. *What types of exercises would be best to achieve my goals?*
3. *How much time can I allot for exercise each day? Each week?*

Consider how similar questions like those above might promote a discussion during a family council:

1. *What kind of "better spiritual shape" do we want?*
2. *What types of exercises would be best to achieve our goals?*
3. *How much time should we allot for these exercises? And when should do them?*

In short, having a goal of "Physical Fitness" and even a "plan" on obtaining it through "diet and exercise," will not produce arrival at the desired destination, unless "diet and exercise" are clearly defined and planned out. An "I'm-not-all-too-concerned-about-the-details" approach toward these fundamental factors is "Alice-like," and while one may be committed and well-meaning, without clear and specific plans they will find themselves falling short of their goal.

The same is true in our quest for spiritual fitness and all the other areas of total fitness. If we hope to get further than just "somewhere" we will need to choose more to do than just "something." The key isn't just choosing to change and doing the right spiritual exercises, it's in measuring our performance and progress along the way.

CHOOSING TO CHANGE | *core concepts*

- Tiger Woods has never been content with his game, even though he's been at the top of his profession for most of the last 20+ years. He's not only made tweaks but has completely disassembled and reconstructed his swing multiple times.

- Progression from one point to another – whether it's intellectual, physical, spiritual, or social – comes at the cost of change we make in our lives.

- Change can be slow and frustrating, monotonous and painful. Ironically, it can also be the most rewarding thing we will ever do.

- We all bring good things from our childhood into adulthood, but we also all bring some "baggage." Baggage can cause us to think, feel, and behave as we were in the past, rather than the person we are striving to become.

- There are a couple types of "crabs" – those who reach up and pull-down people trying to get out of the bucket, or change. Some do this because they feel threatened or question others' sincerity. Others do it out selfishness and insecurity; they don't want to lose a "partner in crime." Those pulling others down whisper with the adversary, "Don't change. You can't change. You won't change. It's too hard to change."

- We often sacrifice the long-term benefits of change and either delay or put it off entirely fearing the short-term learning curve that might accompany it.

- The adversary doesn't care *why* we choose not to change, just that we don't. His objective is to prevent us from receiving blessings, opportunities, spiritual guidance, and become "miserable like unto himself" (2 Ne. 2:27).

- If we hope to get further than just "somewhere" we need to choose more to do than just "something." The key isn't just choosing to change and doing the right exercises, it's in measuring our performance and progress along the way.

Chapter 2

STRATEGIZING FOR SUCCESS

WARNING:
This chapter is going to ask a lot of you and your family. It's going to take more time, thought, and effort than any other chapter in this book. That said, it has the potential to make the most impact as well. So, get after it!

There were 50 other kids in the gym. All were hoping to make the varsity team at Emsley A. Laney High. With only 15 spots on the roster, the reality was that most wouldn't make it. They'd either end up playing for the junior varsity team or be told to go home.

The cards seemed stacked against him. First of all, he was only a sophomore. It was 1978 and very uncommon for varsity teams to take anyone but juniors or seniors on their squad. Second of all, he was only 5'10". While that's not short, it didn't set him apart, by any means. Not only were there plenty of kids trying out that were his height or taller, there were some that were more developed athletically, as well; Michael Jordan couldn't even dunk... yet.

Still, he was determined to make the team. The other 50 kids were, too, but not like Michael. For two weeks, they had all tried hard, hoping that their best effort would catch the eye of the coach and warrant a spot on the roster, but there was something different about him. While Michael wasn't "out-height-ing" or "out-athletic-ing" anyone, he was "out-effort-ing" everyone. He was first in line for all the conditioning drills and ran them as hard as anyone (Kaufmann, 2014). When the conditioning was over and other players wanted another drink, he wanted another drill.

But when the varsity roster was posted, Michael wasn't on it. While it had been duly noted, his relentless effort hadn't been enough. He was crushed. He was listed on the JV roster with many of his fellow sophomores, but that's not what he'd been working for. To add to his frustration, he noticed the varsity list did include one sophomore... it was his good friend, Leroy Smith. Leroy was 6'7". The team had plenty of 5'10" shooters. They needed "length."

Embarrassed and disappointed, Michael went home, locked himself in his room, and cried. Later on, that evening, when his mom came home from work, they cried together. However, the crying would soon end, and those tears would be transformed into liquid motivation. This would come to characterize how Michael would handle any obstacle he'd face throughout his career; create a strategy to figure out how to climb it, go through it, or get around it.

Years later, when asked about being cut, Michael responded, "It`s probably good that it happened." How could being cut from the team be good? "[Because] it made me know what disappointment felt like," he said. "And I knew that I didn`t want to have that feeling ever again" (Green, 1991).

In what would become a lifelong pattern, Michael regrouped after the setback of his sophomore year, doing his part to turn a negative situation into a positive one. Firmly believing that if you strategize (make a plan and do the work), you'll get rewarded, he reset his focus and trained vigorously to prove his worth (it also didn't hurt that he grew 4 inches!). That next season, he made the varsity team and became one of the best high school players in the country. His rapid progress continued as a senior. He averaged a triple double (26.8 points, 11.6 rebounds, and 10.1 assists per game) and was selected to the McDonald's All-American Team.

Michael would continue to have setbacks to respond to. He grew up as an NC State fan and always dreamed of playing there. But when his college recruitment began, he garnered little attention from them. By the time they finally were interested, he'd already signed with the North Carolina Tarheels. After three years in college, Michael decided to enter the NBA draft. Despite having won a national championship, been the recipient of college basketball's prestigious "Wooden Player of the Year Award," and been the leading scorer on the gold medal-winning USA Olympic Basketball team, Michael was chosen third in the 1984 NBA draft. What was the reason those teams passed him over? The same philosophy that was employed back at Laney High: "We already have scorers; we need big men." While he made his presence known early in his NBA career, winning Rookie of the Year, MVP, and multiple scoring titles all within his first 6 seasons, he was unable to lift his teams to any NBA Finals appearances. Critical of his lack of championship appearances, let alone titles, sports writers and pundits called him "selfish" and "one-dimensional." Michael would later lead his teams to six NBA titles, earning the Finals MVP each time.

In a way, the key to Michael's success was failure. If pushed toward a weakness, Michael would turn that weakness into a strength. As a result, he learned to view failure as both a steppingstone and a measuring stick. In keeping with that philosophy, Michael would later summarize his successful basketball career by saying, "I've missed more than 9000 shots in my career. I've lost almost 300 games. 26 times, I've been trusted to take the game winning shot and missed. I've failed over and over and over again in my life. And that is why I succeed" (Middleton, 2016).

Strategizing & Setting Goals

Like Michael, we are all going to face obstacles in our personal and family life. They'll come at us intellectually, physically, spiritually, and socially. Sometimes, we'll fail in our initial effort to overcome them. But if we learn how to use mistakes to our advantage, "each mistake we make can become a lesson in wisdom, turning stumbling blocks into stepping stones" (Robbins, 2018). This is why as individuals and families we must learn to strategize.

A strategy is a plan of action or policy designed to achieve an overall objective. We often hear the term used in sports and in the military, usually to describe the type of intense planning conducted by coaches and officers to put their teams and battalions in the best position to succeed. Likewise, as individuals and families, we need a strategy in place if we're going to succeed in the "game" we're involved in, because everything really is on the line. "[We] need to do better and be better because we are in a battle," taught President Nelson. "The adversary is quadrupling his efforts to disrupt testimonies and impede the work of the Lord. He is arming his minions with potent weapons to keep us from partaking of the joy and love of the Lord" (Nelson, 2019). With our opponent being stronger, the forces of evil raging more fiercely than ever, the days of going into battle without a strategy are long gone. To be successful, individuals and families need to strategize for success.

Setting goals is crucial to our strategizing process. If we don't set goals in life and learn how to master the techniques of living to reach those goals, we will reach only a small part of our full potential. This is true in all the key areas of our development. Remembering the lessons learned from the Cheshire Cat, any approach to a desired destination without goals will only get us "somewhere" (Carroll, 1898). This "somewhere" may be aptly termed, "the Meadow of Mediocrity." We not only need to set goals, but to set meaningful goals that are both measurable and reportable. "It is not enough to want to make the effort and to say we'll make the effort," taught President Monson. "We must *actually* make the effort. It's in the *doing*, not just the *thinking*, that we accomplish our goals. If we constantly put our goals off, we will never see them fulfilled" (Monson, 2007, emphasis added).

The concept of goal setting and achieving isn't a fad or some niche program, it is an essential element of personal growth. Elder Christofferson taught powerfully, "God's ultimate purpose is our progress." He added further, "His desire is that we continue 'from grace to grace, until [we receive] a fulness' of all He can give. That requires more than simply being nice or feeling spiritual" (Christofferson, 2015).

Thus, if we're going to become More Fit 4 the Kingdom and progress from "grace to grace" we need to identify goals and formulate strategies to accomplish this advancement. This often requires change. As outlined in chapter 1, "Choosing to Change," this is essentially what it means to repent – or to steadily improve. "Repentance," said Elder Robbins, "is God's ever-accessible gift that allows and enables us to go from failure to failure without any loss of enthusiasm. Repentance isn't His backup plan in the event we might fail. Repentance is His plan, knowing that we will" (Robbins, 2018).

To put it another way, failure shouldn't only be *expected*, but *accepted*. Michael Jordan not only learned this lesson but how to harness its power – and so must we. To reach our maximum individual or family potential we need to stretch ourselves beyond our current limits. Doing so undoubtedly means some of our efforts will result in failure. But it also means we will know exactly where our limits are and help us in our efforts to expand them!

Thus, getting to a spiritual destination beyond the "Meadow of Mediocrity" will require our very best strategizing and goal-setting efforts. As Michael Jordan would say, "The game [of life] has its ups and downs, but you can never lose focus of your individual goals and you can't let yourself be beat because of lack of effort" (Middleton, 2016).

Creating MOREFIT Goals

As we strategize for success, creating meaningful goals is an essential part of the process. To help provide a framework for successful goal setting and achieving, I created the MOREFIT goal setting and achieving strategy. Combining known patterns and practices with my personal experience, the MOREFIT strategy enables goal setters to refine their goals into clear, achievable, and strategic statements. The strategy utilizes the acronym MOREFIT to capture and emphasize both the key elements of the process and the ultimate outcome: becoming more fit. By framing our goals within this context, we can ensure that our goals are emotionally meaningful and strategic statements of the progress we want to make.

To help explain the MOREFIT goal setting strategy, I'll define each of the components and provide a brief description of each. I'll also present them in the order which best helps create goals, I-R-E-M-T-F-O, rather than M-O-R-E-F-I-T. While certainly not as catchy, following the steps in this order makes goal creation and completion much more effective. Additionally, I'll share pertinent questions to consider for each component. Evaluating and answering these questions ensure that our goals are structured for success. Finally, I'll provide hypothetical examples of an individual working on a physical fitness goal, and a family working on a spiritual goal.

There's a worksheet included at the end of the chapter and the appendix, "The MOREFIT Goal Setting & Achieving Strategy." Make copies of it and practice creating your MOREFIT goals as you read through this chapter:

The MOREFIT Goal Setting & Achieving Strategy

M.O.R.E.F.I.T. | *the acronym*
- Measurable
- One Word-able or One Phrase-able
- Realistic & Reported
- Emotionally Connected
- Fear Confronting & Flexible
- In Writing
- Timely & Tied to an Action

I.R.E.M.T.F.O. | the most effective order
1. In Writing
2. Realistic & Reported
3. Emotionally Connected
4. Measurable
5. Timely & Tied to an Action
6. Fear Confronting & Flexible
7. One Word-able or One Phrase-able

1. MOREFIT | *In writing*

The first step in the MOREFIT strategy is to put our goals in writing. If they aren't written down, they aren't really goals; they're just really nice hopes and dreams. They're also very unlikely of ever being accomplished. There's an old Chinese proverb that states that "the faintest ink is better than the strongest memories." This is absolutely true in our quest to become More Fit 4 the Kingdom.

We have to commit to writing out our goals and revisiting them daily. Ultimately, goals need to be simple, clear, and specific statements, but don't get too hung up on that during this step. The idea here is to just get our hopes and dreams from our head and unto a sheet a paper or device.

Here are some questions to help guide the effort:

1. *What do I want to accomplish and why?*
2. *Will anyone else be involved in accomplishing this or will this be a solo effort?*
3. *When and where will I work on this?*

Physical Example:

- *I want to gain increased physical strength so that I can feel, look, and perform better.*

Spiritual Example:

- *We want to gain more spiritual strength from our Sabbath day and sacrament meeting worship each week.*

Note: Don't worry if you feel your goal doesn't feel like a "finished product" at this point; it shouldn't. This is just step 1. The purpose of the MOREFIT process is to refine your goal step by step. How your goal reads on step 1 will likely be very different than how it reads after step 7.

2. MO**RE**FIT: *Realistic & Reported*

After having put our goals in writing, the next step in the MOREFIT strategy is determine if they're realistic. Goals should require our best efforts. They should represent an increased focus and effort in a specific area. Our goals should require sacrifice, causing us to choose to put aside what we want now for something greater in the future. They should require diligent and consistent effort to achieve. However, if the realization of our goals is dependent upon an unrealistic standard of "diligent and consistent effort," the only thing they'll ever amount to is failure and frustration. The key is to make them both challenging and attainable. Careful consideration is needed to reach that balance.

In addition to being realistic, our MOREFIT goals should be reported. The reporting of our progress can be made to family members, friends, teammates, coworkers, or even via social media. Doing so adds motivational accountability and personal responsibility, providing outside support and encouragement to help us keep at it when inwardly we're ready to give up. Look over the goal statements you wrote down in step 1. Evaluate if they are realistic and consider how you'll report them.

Here are some questions to consider:

1. *Will this goal happen on its own, is it challenging enough?*
2. *Will this single goal occupy all my energy to accomplish, or will it also allow me to work on the meaningful goals I'm setting in the other areas of total fitness?*
3. *How should I report my goals and how often?*
4. *Who should I report to that will be both interested and encouraging?*

Physical Example:

- *Ok, my initial statement was, "I want to gain increased physical strength so that I can feel, look, and perform better." This is realistic; I haven't worked out consistently in months. I think I'll report it to my brother. He's really into fitness and I'll know he'll happy to hear I've started something.*

Spiritual Example:

- *We wrote, "We want to gain more spiritual strength from our Sabbath day and sacrament meeting worship each week." It's definitely realistic – we aren't really doing anything intentionally at the moment to secure those blessings. We'll report our efforts each Monday night as we gather for home evening.*

3. MOREFIT | *Emotionally Connected*

The third step of the MOREFIT strategy is to be emotionally connected to our goals and emotionally confident in our ability to achieve them. To achieve that level of commitment, our goals absolutely have to be *our* goals. It's not that they can't matter to anyone else, or that they can't benefit anyone else. Often, our goals will benefit others and be appreciated by them. It's that if we're doing them *just* for someone else, or *just* for some purpose that we don't fully believe in, it's unlikely we'll stick with it very long. Again, look at the current version of your goal statements and emotionally evaluate what you've written.

Here are a few questions to help determine if we're really feeling connected to the goal we've selected:

1. *Is this something I really want?*
2. *Am I committed to this goal's outcome?*
3. *Do I have the passion and energy to really go after this goal?*

Physical Example:

- *I've been feeling like I've leveled off fitness-wise for a while. I'm know I'm busy, but that's been the excuse for too long. I'm ready to make this happen. I really want to change my shape, put on some muscle. I know that doing so will improve my happiness in other areas as well. Let's do this!*

Spiritual Example:

- *We've been going through the motions for too long. We've heard a lot about the blessings available for honoring the Sabbath and we desperately need them. We're done living beneath our spiritual privileges. Bottom line, we're struggling. We know the Sabbath could and should be a delight; we want to feel that as a family. Even more, we need to...*

4. MOREFIT | *Measurable*

Having a measurable goal is the next step. Measurable goals not only help make our pursuit meaningful, but motivational. Charting progress is extremely inspiring and is essential for long term growth (see Chapter 3). Seeing improvement - or a lack thereof - helps us stay focused, meet deadlines, feel positive pressure to keep working at it, and ultimately enables us to experience the excitement of goal achievement. This is a step where many choose to spend a good amount of time revising their goals. Most fail to factor in measurable components during the initial steps. Now is the time to do so. Make sure to keep the previous steps in mind while making your adjustments, so that the goal remains realistic.

Questions such as these will help determine a goal's measurability:

- *How much? How many? How often? When?*
- *How will I know when it is accomplished? Success will be when _____?*

Physical Example:

- *Alright. Looks like I need to make some revisions to my goal. Things to measure... Ok, I want to increase my strength on the bench press and squat max. I also want to improve my time in the 3-mile run. I'll have to take some strength tests to begin with, but I'll know I've accomplished my goal when*

I can bench 200lbs, squat 300lbs, and run 3 miles in 24 minutes. My new goal statement is:

- *"Through daily morning exercise, I will improve my bench press, squat max, and my 3-mile time so that I can feel, look, and perform better."*

Spiritual Example:

- *Some outward indicators that we can measure will be creating a family plan for Sunday, assigning a different person to be in charge of teaching a "Come Follow Me" lesson each week, and getting to sacrament 10 minutes early. Success will be when we've created the schedule and executed the plan for 6 weeks, giving each member of the family a chance to teach. Our new goal statement is:*

- *"We will strive to gain more spiritual strength from our Sabbath day worship by arriving to sacrament meeting 10 minutes early and by having a 'Come Follow Me' lesson each week after church."*

5. MOREFIT | *Timely & Tied to an Action*

The fifth step of the MOREFIT strategy is to make sure our goals are timely. While they might need to be changed or be modified – which is outlined in step 6 - every goal we set needs a target date. Doing so helps us stay on task and provides another positive pressure to stick with the program. It also helps prevent the "good" and "better" of our everyday tasks from taking priority over our "best," or our higher prioritized goals and efforts.

It's also important to ensure our goals are tied to an action. Identifying key actions may seem obvious, but its another step that's often omitted from the goals people set. We should ensure our goals include the essential action or *"ing"* words to accomplish them. These action words might also be included in the final step of the MOREFIT process, making goals "one word" or "one phrase-able."

Take time to hone your goal statements further by adding both a time and action component to them. Remember that some goals may be completed in a week while realistically, others may require months. Keep those factors in mind as you consider the time and action elements to incorporate into your statements.

Here are some questions to help with those determinations:

1. *When do I want to have achieved this goal?*
2. *Where do I need to be in a week or month from now to get there?*
3. *What action do I need to do on a daily or weekly basis to accomplish this?*
4. *What word best captures the action that I will need to employ to accomplish this?*

Physical Example:

- *My last rewrite looks like this: "I will increase my bench press and squat max and also improve my 3-mile time so that I can feel, look, and perform better." I want to have reached these goals in 3 months. So, I'll test my bench, squat, and 3-mile time next week, then work out 3-month plan. I'll strive to get about 1/3 of the way there each month. My new goal statement will be:*

- *"By charting my progress and exercising daily, I'll improve my bench press, squat max, and my 3-mile time by 1/3 this month to feel, look, and perform better."*

Spiritual Example:

- *Our last family goal statement read like this: "We will to gain more spiritual strength from our Sabbath day worship by arriving to sacrament meeting 10 minutes early and by having a 'Come Follow Me' lesson each week after church." We want to receive these blessings right away, but know we'll need to really give it chance to see if these changes bring the strength we hope. We'll rephrase our goal to read like this:*

- *"By arriving to church 10 minutes early and holding a Sunday afternoon 'Come Follow Me" lesson, we will seek to gain spiritual strength over the next 6 weeks."*

6. MOREFIT | *Fear Confronting & Flexible*

The next step is to ensure that our goal confronts our fears. Some of our goals won't have any "fears" associated with them, but when they do, those fears should be addressed. If not, they will continue to manifest themselves and ultimately paralyze our progress. Our fears don't necessarily need to be the first hurdle we make, but early on we should identify their place on our "track" and strategize how to get over them. By taking small, calculated strides in that direction, getting comfortable with the smaller hurdles before us, we'll recognize that our fears aren't as insurmountable as we may have thought, and we'll build up the strength and confidence required to get over them.

We also need to ensure that our goals are flexible. We need to be prepared to accept that on occasion we're going to encounter legitimate obstacles that will prevent the completion of our goals as we'd originally planned. While our goals should require diligent and consistent effort, and while we should expect bumps along the way, life sometimes sends variables outside our control. When that happens, we don't need to give up or give in, we simply need to give our goals some additional adjustments. We need to evaluate the new situation, modify our course of action, and move forward.

The same is true for goals we're no longer emotionally connected with. If we find we're no longer emotionally driven to accomplish a goal we set just a few weeks ago, we should cross it off the list and move on to a goal that's more meaningful to us.

While it's important to make these considerations initially, especially in regard to confronting fears, it's also important to utilize this step in the weeks that follow. As we start digging into the daily effort of achieving goals, we increase our capacity to identify hurdles we were trying to dodge and goals that we really aren't emotionally connected to.

Here are some questions to help determine if our goals are effectively confronting our fears or if they need to be modified:

1. *What fears do I have in this area of my life? What's preventing my progress in the past?*
2. *What would my life be like if I removed this obstacle?*
3. *Did I incorrectly identify my emotional connection to this goal in the first place or in its importance in the progress I want to make?*

4. *Have circumstances changed sufficiently to justify modification to my goal or will a reasonable diligent and consistent effort still enable me to accomplish it?*

Physical Example:

- *As I think about my goal ("By <u>charting</u> my progress and <u>exercising</u> daily, I will improve my bench press, squat max, and my 3-mile time by 1/3 by the end of the month so I can feel, look, and perform better") I really don't feel any fear about this. I've always enjoyed exercise and I'm not intimidated by the gym. I just really haven't made time for it and have gotten out of the habit. In terms of flexibility, I don't anticipate anything right now. Monday – Friday, 5-6am, I'll be at the gym!*

Spiritual Example:

- *We are scared. We are uncertain. Our goal - "By <u>arriving</u> at church 10 minutes early and <u>holding</u> a Sunday afternoon 'Come Follow Me' lesson, we will seek to gain spiritual strength over the next 6 weeks" - is something we've never even come close to doing before. Not only haven't we done this as a family, my wife and I never did it in the families we grew up in. We just know we need strength to stick together. We're going to give this a shot for the next 6 weeks and see how it goes. We'll be prepared to make adjustments throughout!*

7. MO**R**EFIT | *One Word-able or One Phrase-able*

The final step in the MOREFIT goal setting strategy is take our goal and capture one word or one phrase to represent it. As suggested in step 5, this one word or phrase might be or include the action word we incorporated, but it doesn't have to. Really, this word or phrase can be anything we feel best helps us remember what we're after. Reducing our already honed down goal statement into a single word or phrase helps to identify the essence of our effort. It will create powerful and personal statements that can be easily posted around the house, on our phone's home screen, or on a sticky note at our office at work.

Take a final look at your goals and identify what words and phrases you'll use. Questions such as these will help:

1. *What word or phrase will best help me remember my goal?*
2. *What word or phrase will motivate me the most to achieve my goal?*

Physical Example:

- *"By <u>charting</u> my progress and <u>exercising</u> daily, I will improve my bench press, squat max, and my 3-mile time by 1/3 by the end of the month to feel, look, and perform better"*

- *Strength through Charting & Exercising*

Spiritual Example:

- *"By <u>arriving</u> at church 10 minutes early and <u>holding</u> a Sunday afternoon 'Come Follow Me' lesson, we will seek to gain spiritual strength over the next 6 weeks"*

- *Secure Sabbath Blessings*

A word of caution; when setting individual goals, be careful of those that someone else has power over. For example, "Make the team!" or "receive a revelation" depends on who else tries out or on the timing of the Lord and His wisdom in directing you. But "get in better shape to make the team," or "put myself in better position to be guided by the Spirit," are matters we can control.

The same counsel is true when we set our family goals. While these group efforts inherently involve more than just us, we should set them in a way that the family can control as many of the variables as possible. A goal such as, "We will gather for scriptures as a family for 30 days and then go out for a special family dinner," rather than "We will meet gather for scriptures for 30 *consecutive* days" accomplishes a similar objective - gathering for scripture reading - but takes out a variable that sometimes we can't control: meeting 30 consecutive days.

Perhaps you don't care for a few steps in the MOREFIT goal setting and achieving strategy or you prefer another model that you've had experience with. The key is to find something that works for you. If you've got something going already, stick with it, grow, adapt, and modify it as needed. Remember that any sort of goal-setting process or strategy that becomes too rigid or lacks creativity will fall short of its objective: to help you and your family accomplish something that's been elusive or that you have be otherwise unable to attain.

Summary

No one knows better than us what temptations and weaknesses we're most vulnerable to as individuals and families. Like head coaches and military officers, we can predict and anticipate how the opposition and adversary might try to derail us from reaching our objective. If we have a strategy in place, if we are carefully and deliberately setting and working on accomplishing goals, we will respond effectively when faced with their force.

Now, the particulars of each individual or family's strategies, goals, and plans will differ, both in terms of the exercises employed and the method chosen to track them. Just as in the fitness world there's a wide variety of training styles and tracking methods, so there is in the realm of spiritual fitness. We should carefully and prayerfully strategize and game plan about our spiritual fitness efforts. While the principles of gaining strength apply to both the physical and spiritual realm, there's not "one" method of strategizing - choosing exercises, charting progress, and measuring success - that's right for everyone. Just as our challenges, interests, and preferences change over time – so should the ways we go about strategizing for them.

APPLICATION & DISCUSSION | CH 2 | 1.0

See a blank "The MOREFIT Goal Setting & Achieving Strategy" worksheet at the end of this chapter and in the appendix. Make a copy and create your own MOREFIT goals. For a starting point, consider the things you identified back in the introduction (Application & Discussion: Introduction | 1.0). Consider the items you noted in the "Start, Stop, and Continue" questions you answered there. Refer to the questions and examples illustrated in this chapter as you go.

STRATEGIZING FOR SUCCESS | *core concepts*

- Like Michael Jordan, we are going to face obstacles and opposition in our personal and family life. Sometimes we will fail in our effort to overcome them. We can use that information to strategize to our advantage.

- If we don't set goals in life and learn the techniques needed to reach those goals, we will only reach a small part of our full potential.

- Failure shouldn't only be expected but accepted. To reach our maximum potential we need to stretch ourselves beyond our current limits.

- Goals should be written down and revisited daily. If they aren't in writing, they aren't really goals. They're just really nice hopes and dreams.

- Goals should realistic, striking the balance between challenging and attainable. If the realization of our goals is dependent on an unrealistic standard, the only thing they enable us to achieve is failure and frustration. Reporting our progress creates support and accountability to keep going when we may want to give up.

- Goals should be emotionally connected to our efforts at improvement. They need to be something we want and believe it.

- Goals should measurable. Measurable goals not only help make our pursuit meaningful, but motivation. Charting progress is extremely inspiring and essential for long term growth.

- Goals should have a target date for measurement and/or completion. Having a date provides positive pressure to stick with the program. Goals should also be tied to an action essential to achieving them.

- Goals should confront our fears. Taking small, calculated steps toward them will eventually get us over them. We need to be prepared to accept that on occasion we will have to be flexible with our goals, strategize, modify, and adjust them.

- If we have a strategy in place, if we are carefully and deliberately setting and working on accomplishing goals, we will respond effectively when faced with their force.

APPLICATION & DISCUSSION: CHAPTER 2 | 1.0
The MOREFIT Goal Setting & Achieving Strategy

Luke 2:52	1. In Writing 2. Realistic & Reported 3. Emotionally Connected 4. Measurable
	5. Timely & Tied to an Action 6. Fear Confronting & Flexible 7. One Word or One Phrase-able

WISDOM INTELLECTUAL	1:
	2:
	3:
	4:
	5:
	6:
	7:

STATURE PHYSICAL	1:
	2:
	3:
	4:
	5:
	6:
	7:

FAVOR WITH GOD SPIRITUAL	1:
	2:
	3:
	4:
	5:
	6:
	7:

FAVOR WITH MAN SOCIAL	1:
	2:
	3:
	4:
	5:
	6:
	7:

Chapter 3

MEASURING PERFORMANCE

"Find a way." That's the mantra Diana Nyad adopted for her final attempt to do something no human had ever done before. Diana was hoping to swim 103 miles from Cuba to Florida without a protective cage!

This wasn't her first attempt trying to find a way. In fact, it was her fifth. Over a span of 35 years, Diana had been trying to "find a way." She'd failed every time. She wanted just one more shot.

When Diana made her first attempt in 1978, she was only 28 years old. While young, she'd already proven herself as a world-class distance swimmer. During her initial effort, she swam inside a 20-by-40-foot steel shark cage. While the cage protected her from lurking sea creatures, strong Westerly winds and 8-foot swells slammed against it and pushed her off course. She'd covered an impressive 76 miles but had to be removed from the water 42 hours into her swim. She'd never use a cage again.

While Diana would set a world record in 1979, a 102-mile swim from Bimini, Bahamas, to Jupiter, Florida, she wouldn't make her second attempt at the Cuba to Florida swim until 2011; 33 years after her first effort. Opting out of the security of the shark cage, she chose to swim assisted by an electronic "Shark Shield" – a system that sends electrical pulses through the water functioning much like an electric fence for dogs, only in this case, hoping to keep the sharks at bay. Despite her strategic improvements, she was unable to reach her destination. Twenty-nine hours into her swim, she had to be pulled from the water. Strong winds that had pushed her miles off course were part of the problem, but that wasn't what stopped her. It wasn't the shoulder pain she'd been suffering since hour 3, either. Ironically, it was something she'd dealt with her whole life; asthma. Her breathing became so constricted during her last hour in the water that she could barely manage a few strokes before having to stop to catch her breath. Once again, Diana couldn't find a way.

Her third attempt came later in that same year, 2011. No steel cages. No winds. No asthma. Things seemed to be going well. However, 41 miles in she encountered a new obstacle; Jellyfish and Portuguese man-of-war. It wasn't the many stings to her forearms and neck that slowed her progress. She was prepared to fight through that. It was the respiratory distress caused by her body's reaction to the stings. Despite her desire to swim on, she had to end her swim prematurely, once again.

Diana's fourth attempt came in 2012. This time she managed to cover more mileage than any of her earlier attempts. Unfortunately, two bad storms and nine jellyfish stings – both foes she'd faced before – combined against her, forcing her to abandon her swim.

For most people, all these failures would be reason to give up the cause. But when interviewed in Florida following her fourth failure, Diana said: "I do not feel like a failure at all. But we needed a little more luck" (Moore, 2011). And so, Diana and her team set out to try again.

Diana's refusal to see her previous efforts as failures enabled her to prepare more effectively. Valuable measurements were made of each attempt, both in terms of the dangers along the way and in regard to her mental and physical well-being during the various stages of the route. Strategies were analyzed and improved to compensate for gaps in conditioning and in dealing with the obstacles she would face. And of course, they'd hope "luck" would cooperate!

Consequently, for her fifth attempt, Diana wore surgical gloves and a prosthetic mask. This limited the impact jellyfish and man-of-war stings could have on her. Additionally, she was accompanied by a 35-member crew and two sailboats. They monitored her health, updated the world on her progress via social media, and also swam out ahead to help ward off sharks and clear the path of jellyfish. As a result, on Monday, September 2, 2013, Diana Nyad became the first person to swim from Cuba to Florida without a protective cage! She had swum a mind-boggling 53 consecutive hours. Even more impressive, Diana was 64 years old!

Still, despite all her training, preparation, and research, it was in no way an easy swim. There were many times that it seemed she'd have to be pulled from the water. At one point, the large amounts of saltwater she'd swallowed caused excessive vomiting. At another, she was shivering so bad from the cold she could barely swim. Add to that the extreme physical and mental fatigue such an arduous quest would cause anyone, and don't mind the fact that she was 64 years old! Nevertheless, Diana pushed through it all. She made it. She had kept repeating her mantra in her head: "Find a way. Find a way. Find a way."

After pumping her fist in the air (and before being guided into an ambulance) Diana shared these three messages with those who'd gathered to cheer her on: "One is we should never, ever give up. Two is you're never are too old to chase your dreams. Three is it looks like a solitary sport, but it's a team" (Myre, 2013). Diana had found a way!

Measuring & Reporting Performance

Like Diana Nyad, our "swim" isn't going to be easy. Our path will be fraught with the spiritual equivalent of Westerly winds, 8-foot swells, shivering waters, sharks, and jellyfish. We're going to have many failed attempts along the way. However, if we learn to gather and chart that data, the record of our past failures can become the reason for our future success. As President Thomas S. Monson taught, "When performance is measured, performance improves. When performance is measured and reported, the rate of improvement accelerates" (Monson, 1970).

This oft-used quotation was initially given during a talk in 1970 while introducing a new teacher development program. It was shared in reference to the program's implementation and how General Authorities would be visiting each stake then giving a report back to the Brethren in regard to the program's progress. While most of that original content isn't applicable here, the stated goal of the program is fitting to the topic at hand. Using "More Fit 4 the Kingdom" as substitute for "teaching" the correlation is clear: "The basic goal of [becoming More Fit 4 the Kingdom] is to help bring about worthwhile changes in the lives of boys and girls, men and women. The aim is to inspire the individual to think about, feel about, and then do something about living gospel principles" (Monson, 1970).

Consider how that old Sunday school objective aligns with the vision of the new initiative for children and youth: "Strengthen the rising generations faith in Jesus Christ, help children, youth, and their families progress along the covenant path as they meet life's challenges" (Church, 2019). The focus remains the same!

Many lessons could be learned from the example of Diana and her team. For starters, they had a clear goal in mind. Just getting "somewhere" was out of the question. Second, they developed a detailed strategy and game plan on how to achieve it. That plan included studying weather patterns and water currents, pushing the limits on physical conditioning and the use of modern technology to assist in their effort. Third, they meticulously recorded the result of their efforts, turning "stumbling blocks into stepping stones."

While we likely won't have a 35-man team, nor hundreds of thousands of dollars at our disposal, we can follow a similar strategy and pattern of preparation. If not, it really doesn't matter what our goal is or what system we used to set it. Without a plan and a way to track and measure where we've been, where we're at, and where we're going, we will be very unlikely to "find a way." Run, lift, walk, swim, or bike? Work out three, four, or five times a week? It doesn't matter. While some progress *might* be made with a haphazard approach, it definitely won't be the progress that *could* have been made.

Keeping a Logbook

Now, the introduction of any sort of exercise will always be met initially with increased health and performance. This will happen whether a plan has been created or not and regardless of whether it's being tracked and recorded. In this sense, change is initially much like jumping into cold water; anything will be a shock, at first. But after a while "in the water," we all begin to adapt to the coldness. Now, adaptation isn't always bad. Things that were once intimidating can become approachable and things that were once painful can become invigorating. However, a random unchecked plan of continually just "jumping into the pool" and "splashing around" will quickly plateau without a method of charting progression (see chapter 4, "The Overload Principle," for more information on "adaptation").

Therefore, in order to become More Fit 4 the Kingdom, keeping some sort of log book is essential. Doing so aids both in assessing progress and in providing motivation to stick with the program. Just as was discussed in chapter 2 in regard to goals, recording our efforts enables us to effectively plan ahead and strategize where we can be in a week, a month, or more. It also allows us to see how far we've come and whether or not we've plateaued.

Effective physical fitness workout logs include the date, the lifts completed along with the number of sets and repetitions, the amount of weight used for each lift, and any other comments for the day, such as general feelings about the workout. If we did 3 sets of 15 push-ups last week for a total of 45 push-ups, having it recorded will enable us to target 46-50 total push-ups over the next couple of weeks in order to become a little stronger. If we did squats with 185 pounds on the bar last week, our next goal will need to be squatting 186-

200 pounds or more, and so forth. The process of adding a little more weight each time is called the "Overload Principle" and will be more fully outlined in chapter 4. Following the practice of recording progress provides purpose to workouts, evidence of increased fitness, and motivation to continue putting our body through the discomfort that is bringing increased strength and conditioning.

"I just don't get much out of it."

When a person who is set on losing 10 pounds and who has been dieting and exercising for weeks notices no change to the scale, they begin to reason, "Why should I rearrange my schedule to get to the gym and restrict myself from all my favorite foods when I don't get much out of it anyway!?" The same is true for someone pursuing a spiritual fitness goal. "Why should I get up early to sacrifice time and sleep to study the scriptures when I don't get much out of it anyway?" I call this condition "scripture reading fatigue." Many also develop "prayer fatigue," or "marital communication fatigue," or "professional development fatigue," and so on. While in most cases, following the instructions outlined for the MOREFIT goal setting and achieving strategy prevent this from happening in most cases, sometimes our best efforts just don't yield the results we're hoping for. Anytime we set goals to improve only to find little to no success, we are prone to experience this sort of fatigue.

In April 2011, Elder Ballard shared a story that perfectly illustrates this scenario. The story features a young merchant from Boston who, in 1849, was caught up in the fervor of the California gold rush. He sold all of his possessions to seek his fortune in the California rivers, which he was told were "filled with gold nuggets so big that one could hardly carry them." The story reads as follows:

> "Day after endless day, the young man dipped his pan into the river and came up empty. His only reward was a growing pile of rocks. Discouraged and broke, he was ready to quit until one day an old, experienced prospector said to him, 'That's quite a pile of rocks you are getting there, my boy.'

> "The young man replied, 'There's no gold here. I'm going back home.'

> "Walking over to the pile of rocks, the old prospector said, 'Oh, there is gold all right. You just have to know where to find it.' He picked two rocks up in his hands and crashed them together. One of the rocks split open, revealing several flecks of gold sparkling in the sunlight.

> "Noticing a bulging leather pouch fastened to the prospector's waist, the young man said, 'I'm looking for nuggets like the ones in your pouch, not just tiny flecks.'

> "The old prospector extended his pouch toward the young man, who looked inside, expecting to see several large nuggets. He was stunned to see that the pouch was filled with thousands of flecks of gold.

> "The old prospector said, 'Son, it seems to me you are so busy looking for large nuggets that you're missing filling your pouch with these precious flecks of gold.

The patient accumulation of these little flecks has brought me great wealth'" (Ballard, 2011).

It's clear that the young man in this story wanted to find treasure. It's also evident he was willing to follow a plan to get it. However, while he knew he was looking for gold, he was only trained to recognize and value it in one form; gold nuggets.

His frustration came in the same manner that our struggle with scripture study often does. We don't get much out of it because we can't figure out where the "gold" is or how to find it - unless it comes in the form of a large nugget. Additionally, when we have found it, we don't value it much because it doesn't live up to the single standard of measurement we've adopted and defined as "successful scripture study." In essence, we throw all "non-nugget" discoveries to the ground shouting, "I'm not interested in those tiny flecks!" While we desire the promise of the prophets that as we ponder what we've studied, the "windows of heaven will open, and [we] will receive answers to [our] own questions and direction for [our] own [lives] – we don't know what to do when that desired "nugget" outcome manifests itself in the "tiny fleck" form we hadn't anticipated" (Nelson, 2017).

Learning to Identify, Measure, and Value the "Gold"

Now, we could substitute "scripture study" with any other worthy goal in our overall fitness quest; success in school, our physical strength or appearance, our closeness to the Spirit, or our relationships with family and friends. Like the young merchant in the story who had actually made daily discoveries of valuable tiny flecks of gold, it's easy to feel like we aren't getting anywhere when in fact we've actually made meaningful progress. We need to be careful not to use a single and potentially inaccurate standard of measurement to define our efforts as either a "success" or "failure."

Those in the physical fitness world face a similar challenge. Perhaps due to tradition, cultural acceptance, or convenience, the scale often becomes, for many, the lone measurement standard they look to. In many instances the scale becomes their source of validation - the "gold nugget." Consequently, the scale can cause the fitness seeker to become overly excited if their weight is lower, and unreasonably depressed if their weight is higher. While the scale *can* serve as an effective measurement, it isn't the *only* tool of measurement. Even more, in many cases it may not be the right tool. Keep this in mind; panning for gold is only effective if you're near a river. But a river isn't the only place you can find gold! The scale can cause the fitness seeker to feel unsuccessful when in reality they've actually experienced significant change in body composition and their overall physical fitness.

Many women that strength train report that their weight has increased. This is due to the increased muscle they've gained. Tape measurements of their legs and arms might show they've actually decreased in circumference, yet despite this being the outcome they wanted (decreased size), their gains are cast aside as they look at the scale and sadly conclude, "my training isn't working; I must be doing something wrong!" Having placed the scale as their "gold nugget" standard of measurement, they look past what the patient accumulation of tiny fitness gains could bring them over time: significant improvement in personal fitness and appearance.

Thus, those seeking to effectively measure physical fitness gains don't totally abandon the scale, but they include other measures of fitness to help track their progress. Such examples include getting up the courage to take pictures each month in front of the mirror (super scary and revealing, but extremely effective), taking monthly tape measurements of key areas of the body, measuring body fat percentage, or simply - and perhaps most effectively – using actual fitness gains as the measurement: they can run faster or further, push or pull more weight, or jump higher or quicker than before.

The same is true in our other areas of development. When we define individual success in school to only mean, "I earned A's," success in work as, "I received a promotion," and success in social life as, "I got 100 likes on Instagram," we're setting ourselves up for failure. Likewise, when we define family success to mean only things like "all my kids were accepted to this College," or "my son got his mission call right out of high school," we're setting ourselves up for failure and are likely guilty of measuring the wrong things. It's not that measurements like these couldn't be meaningful indicators of our efforts, it's that they don't show a complete picture of them, and in many instances wouldn't be the most effective measurement standard at all.

A person who has tracked and recorded their sets and reps will have much better evidence than the scale can provide of their fitness accomplishments: "I ran a 9-minute mile last month and now I'm running a mile in 8 minutes!" "Last month I could do 8 pull-ups and now I can do 10!" "I did the same circuit today I did last month but was able to complete it 90 seconds faster!" Indicators such as these may or may not show up on the scale but are highly accurate measurements of a person's overall fitness improvements.

This same challenge is also faced by those seeking to become more spiritually fit. Going back to the scripture reading example, the reason many feel like they aren't getting anything out of their personal scripture study is because they've only learned to look for big "nuggets." The desire is there. The plan is there. The effort is there. But outside of the "what stands out to me?" search technique most people come naturally equipped with, they lack additional tools and understanding of how to "prospect through and dig into the scriptures like a miner searching for precious metal" (Packer, 1989). Like the physical fitness seeker only using the scale to judge their results, those seeking spiritual fitness need to learn to look beyond "gold nugget discovery." Individuals and families seeking to become More Fit 4 the Kingdom in all areas of fitness need to go beyond the equivalent of the commonly accepted rubric of scripture readers: "pages read per day." Measurements like these are like unto a gold miner saying, "I'm going to stick my pan in the river 20 times today... period." While a nugget could end up in their pan, the chances are most days he'll come up empty in his efforts.

This is where full-blown "fatigue" can take place in our lives. Whether in our intellectual, physical, spiritual, or social efforts, when our progress stalls, so does our desire to carry on. While we might be able to overcome short stretches of time without meaningful accomplishment and still find the resolve to keep trying, continual exposure to a pattern of feeling unsuccessful in our efforts will wear down the desire of even the most diligent pursuer. As a result, commitment to our daily quest for overall fitness that once seemed so concrete can be compromised.

Something More than Reading

If when we arrive at the seemingly less-spectacular passages, we haven't learned to extract the "gold," our motivation to search the next day will be weakened. Like the young prospector, we can find ourselves on the brink of giving up altogether. Elder Christofferson described a more effective way to track "gold nugget" and "gold fleck" discovery and how to measure our scripture study success when he taught:

> "When I say 'study,' I mean something more than reading. It is a good thing sometimes to read a book of scripture within a set period of time to get an overall sense of its message, but for conversion, you should care more about the amount of time you spend in the scriptures than about the amount you read in that time. I see you sometimes reading a few verses, stopping to ponder them, carefully reading the verses again, and as you think about what they mean, praying for understanding, asking questions in your mind, waiting for spiritual impressions, and writing down the impressions and insights that come so you can remember and learn more. Studying in this way, you may not read a lot of chapters or verses in a half hour, but you will be giving place in your heart for the word of God, and He will be speaking to you. Remember Alma's description of what it feels like: 'It beginneth to enlarge my soul; yea, it beginneth to enlighten my understanding, yea, it beginneth to be delicious to me.' You will know that the gospel is being written in your heart, that your conversion is happening, as the word of the Lord from His prophets, past and present, feels

more and more delicious to your soul" (Christofferson, 2004).

In this comparison, Elder Christofferson puts more emphasis on alternate measurements of scriptural study success than he does the number of pages we read. These measurements include the amount of time, the level of pondering, the incorporation of prayer, the asking and recording of questions, the waiting and receiving of revelation. Like unto the many physical gains that don't show up on a scale, these spiritual gains don't show up in terms of "pages per day." Nevertheless, they are significantly more meaningful and applicable in measuring our spiritual progression and provide tangible motivation to the one seeking for treasure.

APPLICATION & DISCUSSION | CH 3 | 1.0
Evaluate your personal and family scripture study plan and consider how you can make it more effective:

1. *Am I more worried about turning pages, or turning my heart toward God?*

   _____

2. *Am I just reading, or am I taking time to ponder what I'm studying?*

   _____

3. *Am I praying for understanding before, during, or after I study?*

   _____

4. *Am I asking questions and recording questions I have?*

   _____

5. *Am I seeking revelation as part of my study?*

    _____

6. *How I plan to measure my scripture study moving forward:*

    _____

    _____

7. *What other spiritual exercises could I incorporate into my life?*

    _____

    _____

    _____

    _____

(For a blank copy of this "Application & Discussion" see the Appendix)

Preparing for Setbacks

Every athlete knows that injury and sickness are a part of sport. Remember Diana Nyad's experience; large waves crashing against her, ever changing wind patterns, ocean storms, asthma, jellyfish stings, and potential shark attacks to name a few. As outlined in chapter 2, we need to be flexible (see chapter 2, Strategizing for Success). There are sometimes things that are just out of our control. Even with our best strategies and plans in place, life just happens. We won't make it to the gym. We'll miss a day of scripture reading. We'll carefully plan out a Sabbath day plan for the family only to have it fall apart and fail miserably. Don't quit. Don't let those variables become dead ends and, like the young merchant from Boston, want to quit in frustration. Rather, keep at it and, like Diana Nyad, "Find a way!"

I experienced this personally a few years ago. My wife and I undertook to run a full marathon – 26.2 miles. Prior to that decision, neither of us had run competitively at any level.

We hadn't even competed recreationally in any 5k, 10k, or half-marathon events. But it was something we wanted to do and something we could do together. So, we went after it. Ultimately, we'd ended up training for three full marathons together over a three-year period! It was an amazing experience. But after the third marathon, I had to call it quits. I'd developed plantar fasciitis in both feet so bad that getting out of bed in the morning and planting my feet on the ground felt like I had hammers crashing down on my heels! It seemed like overnight I went from being able to run long distances every weekend to being unable to bear the pain of a quarter-mile run. It was devastating.

However, a great friend of mine, who is also an amazing Physical Therapist Assistant (PTA), helped me understand that I could run again someday, but that it would take some work. He taught me stretches that I needed to incorporate into my regimen, found me the right inserts for my shoes, and worked on my feet twice a week for about 6 months. During that time, I continued to exercise, but I had to change up my routine. The weightlifting was fine, doing squats and other leg-focused lifts didn't hurt at all, but running was problematic. I had to figure out a different way to keep up on my cardio.

Consequently, I chose to change. I strategized. I modified the way I had been doing box jumps. Instead of quickly jumping up and going down, I'd jump up to maintain my explosive strength and then carefully lower myself to the floor. Instead of focusing on repetitions, I focused on height. Additionally, I researched how to use the rowing machine and introduced it into my regimen. I substituted rowing for what had been 10, 15, and 20-minute running bouts. It helped me to simulate sustained and static cardio, like I experienced on a long run, all while not hurting my feet. Finally, I incorporated swimming more intensely than I had before. I found that by swimming sprint intervals I could duplicate the anaerobic gains that running sprints brought, all while eliminating the stress that running put on my feet.

As a result of the strategies I employed - therapy, the modification of certain exercises, and the introduction of others - my feet were not only healed and strengthened to the point I could run distance without pain, but I became capable of performing other physical feats I wasn't even considering before. I can now jump higher, row further, and swim faster than ever before. And just recently I ran my first race since my injury, a half-marathon (13.1 miles). I completed it with a PR better than 30 seconds per mile faster than my previous best run!

Learning from Setbacks

Like Diana Nyad's experience with swimming and mine with running, we need to learn to accept that trials and setbacks can be part of our progression. Of course, this is as true in the spiritual realm as it is in the physical. "Success," it has been said, "isn't the absence of failure, but *going* and *growing* from failure to failure without any loss of enthusiasm" (Robbins, 2018). To prepare for the kingdom we are seeking to become more fit for, we must be proved and tested, "to see if [we] will do all things whatsoever the Lord their God shall command [us]" (Abraham 3:25). Sometimes in our strivings we seek to "pray away" the plan of salvation, wishing to avoid all the challenges before us, rather than be strengthened in them or by them.

Nephi understood that there'd be setbacks along the way to becoming More Fit 4 the Kingdom. As he and his family struggled in their strivings, he found himself bound with cords by his own brothers, deserted in the wilderness with the intent of being devoured by wild beasts. Certainly, this wasn't part of his MOREFIT strategy! "But it came to pass that I prayed," said Nephi, "O Lord, according to my faith which is in thee, wilt thou deliver me from the hands of my brethren; yea, even *give me strength* that I may burst these bands with which I am bound. And it came to pass that when I had said these words, behold, the bands were loosed from off my hands and feet" (1 Nephi 7:16-18, emphasis added).

Sister Wendy W. Nelson reminded us that we came to Earth to be tested. While acknowledging that the testing would be painful, she added this promising insight:

> "I believe if you could remember who you said you would help while you are here on earth, or what anguishing experiences you agreed to go through, that whatever really tough situation you are presently in — or will be in—you would say, 'Oh, now I remember. Now I understand. This difficult situation makes sense to me now. With the Lord's help I can do this!'" (Nelson, Hope of Israel, 2018).

Thus, tests are a part of the mortal experience, essential to gaining strength and experience, so why would we try to pray them away – to be exempt – or seek to be? Added resistance is key to incremental growth (see chapter 4, "The Overload Principle"). While we may not know which challenges God has caused or merely has permitted in our lives, we can know He's aware of them. Interestingly, Elder Pace taught, "[Often] trials and tribulations are allowed to come into [our lives] because of what [we] are doing right" (Pace, 1987). Whatever the source of our trials, we will all be aided in our fitness quest to apply the following admonition:

"When these trials come, the adversary's minions begin broadcasting that you did something wrong, that this is a punishment, a sign that Heavenly Father does not love you. Ignore that!" (Klebingat, 2014). Indeed, we should accept setbacks as a time to prove ourselves and partner with the Lord in enduring to the end.

Choosing How to Chart

There are many techniques and tools available to teach and assist how to track our progress as individuals and families. Utilizing a goal setting and achieving strategy like MOREFIT is a good place to start, but that process is designed to create and achieve goals; a tracking system, logbook, or journal is needed to track our efforts along the way. A simple search on Google or the app store of a smartphone will likely yield dozens of excellent options. What's essential isn't *how* we choose to track our goals and plans, only that we *do*. Selecting the right tool as a goal-tracking system will not only help us in our efforts, but significantly increase the likelihood of accomplishing them.

Here are some basic tips to consider when choosing how to chart:

1. Select a tracking system that is easy to use and doesn't require a lot of time to learn and set up. The purpose of the tool is to help focus on our efforts to accomplish our goals, not to learn myriads of features or functions associated with a fancy app! If a particular tool or tracking system doesn't seem to work for you, abandon it!

2. Select a tracking system that incorporates the goals you've already labored to identify, hone down, and create.

Whether you've chosen to set and achieve your goals following the MOREFIT strategy or some other method, find a tracking system than works with it. Setting your goals should be the heavy lifting of your organizational efforts; the tracking system you choose to carry them out should be light work. It's a tool for tracking, it should help you see where you're at, to return to your goal statements and evaluate if you're on track.

3. Select a tracking system that incorporates some method of journaling. Journaling enables you to easily evaluate progress and adjust our goals if needed. These journal entries don't need to be long or detail, although they could be. For physical fitness goals, you'll want a place to record numerical and time measurements, like your reps and weight. For spiritual goals though, you might want a place to right more personal insights like, "I found this today while reading," or "While in the temple I learned." Such entries allow us to look back and actually see the results we were working for, thus motivating us to continue moving forward.

While the style and function of each tracking system will vary, they are all fueled by the same thing: action. They support and encourage our personal initiative – they don't replace it. Without action, no matter how effectively a MOREFIT a goal is structured or how well it's managed, it will never be achieved.

Summary

There is an immense payoff for our commitment to measuring our efforts in becoming More Fit 4 the Kingdom. As we record the incremental yet life-altering changes in who we are and the direction our life is taking, we not only better recognize the hand of God and His tender mercies in our lives but become better motivated to continue our increased performance and productivity. President Harold B. Lee detailed this pattern when he said:

> "The most important of all the commandments of God is that one that you are having the most difficulty keeping today. If it is one of dishonesty, if it is one of unchastity, if it is one of falsifying, not telling the truth, today is the day for you to work on that until you have been able to conquer that weakness. Put that aright and then you start on the next one that is most difficult for you to keep. That's the way to sanctify yourself by keeping the commandments of God" (Williams, 1996, p.82).

The results of this process are a continual chain of goals accomplished. The success won't be because we progress forward free of mistakes and setbacks. Rather, the success will be the increased evidence God's power we see in our lives as we do our best and feel the Savior encircle us in the arms of His everlasting love (2 Ne. 1:15).

MEASURING PERFORMANCE | *core concepts*

- Like Diana Nyad, our swim isn't going to be easy. Our path will be fraught with difficulty and failure. But if we learn to gather and chart those experiences, the record of our past failures can become the reason for our future successes.

- While some progress might be made without a strategy, it definitely won't be the progress that could have been made with one.

- Keeping a logbook of some sort is essential. Doing so enables us to effectively plan ahead and strategize where we can be in a week, a month, or more. It allows us to see how far we've come and whether or not we've plateaued.

- We develop fatigue and the desire to quit any time our strategies to improve yield little to no success.

- We need to be careful not to use a single and potentially inaccurate standard of measurement to define our efforts as either a "success" or "failure."

- Sometimes there are things that are just out of our control. Even with our best strategies and plans in place, life just happens. Don't let those variables become dead ends. Don't quit! Find a way!

- Choose to chart! What's essential isn't how you choose to track your progress, only that you do. Selecting the right tool for you or your family will help to clarify, simplify, and carry out your goals.

- The most important of all God's commandments is the one you are having the most difficulty keeping. Figure out what that is, make that weak things strong. Move on to the next weakness. Repeat. That's the process

Chapter 4
THE OVERLOAD PRINCIPLE

Milo of Croton was a famous wrestler and one of the most illustrious athletes of ancient Greece. Born over 2,000 years ago in an ancient Greek colony of southern Italy, he won the Olympic wrestling championship six times in the 6th century BC. So great was his strength that once, as legend has it, when a building collapsed, he supported the roof while his friends escaped unharmed! (Britannica, 2017).

While stories differ, it is generally told that Milo gained his great strength by following a training program from his youth to manhood. As a boy, Milo was given a bull calf to raise and care for. Each day, Milo's father asked him, "How big is your bull today?" At that, Milo would run outside, pick up the calf, and carry him inside to show his father. Other variations have Milo carrying the calf up a hill or around a field. Each day this pattern continued – "Milo, how big is your bull?" and Milo would lift him in his arms, carry him on his back, or hoist him upon his shoulders and bring him in. This went on for years. Since the bull grew up only gradually, Milo did not notice the change in its weight. As the bull grew, so did Milo's strength. He could easily lift it in his arms even when it grew into an adult bull. This enabled him to become an athlete of unparalleled strength and stamina.

Progressive Resistance

While the story may be nothing more than a myth, it does contain a very important training message. In order for us to gain impressive levels of strength, we need to follow a program of progressive resistance for an extended period of time. Today, this same concept is known as "The Overload Principle."

The overload principle is the basic concept behind all workouts. In order for a muscle to increase strength, it must be gradually stressed by working against a load greater than it is accustomed to. To increase endurance, muscles must work for a longer period of time than they are used to or at a higher intensity. As a result, the body's various systems adjust and increase their capacity to perform physical work. Over time, one can improve their physical strength, endurance, quickness, or agility by gradually increasing their workload.

Spiritual strength is gained in similar fashion; gradually and steadily increasing the load we are accustomed to carrying. As the scriptures teach, "[By] small and simple things are great things brought to pass" (Alma 37:6). Elder Eyring explained the overload principle this way, saying:

> "My experience has taught me this about how people and organizations improve: the best place to look is for small changes we could make in things we do often. There is power in steadiness and repetition. And if we

can be led by inspiration to choose the right small things to change, consistent obedience will bring great improvement" (Eyring, 2004).

Milo of Croton is proof of that! Yet, adding an increased load to our already busy personal and family lives seems like the last thing we would want to do, right? True, life can become cluttered with too many "good" things at the cost of the "best" things. However, we should be careful not to confuse the important role of carrying a meaningful load with being too busy. "[Bearing] a load is a necessary and essential part of the plan of happiness" (Bednar, 2014).

Elder Bednar expounded upon this principle, sharing a story about a man who went to cut wood in the forest on a winter day. Having parked his truck in the desired location, he realized he was stuck in the deep snow. After multiple efforts, he recognized that he did not know what to do to extricate himself from this dangerous situation. Wanting to do more than just sit there, he climbed out of the vehicle and started cutting wood. He completely filled the back of the truck with the heavy load and then determined he would try driving out of the snow one more time. As he put the pickup into gear and applied power, he started to inch forward. Slowly the truck moved out of the snow and back onto the road. He finally was free to go home, a happy and humbled man. Elder Bednar then explained:

> "Each of us also carries a load. Our individual load is comprised of demands and opportunities, obligations and privileges, afflictions and blessings, and options and constraints. Two guiding questions can be helpful as we periodically and prayerfully assess our load: 'Is the load I am carrying producing the spiritual traction

that will enable me to press forward with faith in Christ on the strait and narrow path and avoid getting stuck? Is the load I am carrying creating sufficient spiritual traction so I ultimately can return home to Heavenly Father?'...

"Sometimes we mistakenly may believe that happiness is the absence of a load. But bearing a load is a necessary and essential part of the plan of happiness. Because our individual load needs to generate spiritual traction, we should be careful to not haul around in our lives so many nice but unnecessary things that we are distracted and diverted from the things that truly matter most" (Bednar, 2014).

APPLICATION & DISCUSSION | CH 4 | 1.0
Answer the questions posed by Elder Bednar:

1. *Is the load I'm carrying producing the needed spiritual traction to enable me to press forward with faith in Christ on the strait and narrow path and avoid getting stuck?*

_____

_____

_____

_____

2. *Is the load I am carrying creating sufficient spiritual traction so I ultimately can return home to Heavenly Father?*

_____

_____

_____

_____

3. *How about as a family – do we have the spiritual traction needed to stick together through the challenges that lie ahead?*

_____

_____

_____

_____

(For a blank copy of this "Application & Discussion" see the Appendix)

It should be noted that it's only through the Savior's Atonement that we can receive capacity and "strength beyond [our] own" needed to draw closer to Him (Church, Hymns, #220). As the Lord declared:

"Come unto me, all ye that labour and are heavy laden, and I will give you rest…Take my yoke upon you, and learn of me; for I am meek and lowly in heart: and ye shall find rest unto your souls…For my yoke is easy, and my burden is light" (Matt 11:28-30).

Latter-day Teachings on the Overload Principle

Variations of this concept have been taught repeatedly in recent years, as well. Here's a sampling of notable quotes teaching similar principles:

- "…if you feel small and weak, please simply come unto Christ, who makes weak things strong. The weakest among us, through God's grace, can become spiritually strong, because God 'is no respecter of persons'" (Uchtdorf, 2010)

- "Small efforts sustained over time can produce significant results" (Durrant, 2015)

- "We do not have to be perfect, but we need to be good and getting better. We need to strive to live the plain and simple truths of the gospel" (Clark, 2015)

Closely associated with the overload principle are the principles of "progression" and "adaptation." An examination of both will help shed light on further application in one's quest to become More Fit 4 the Kingdom.

Progression

Progression implies that there is an optimal level of overload that should be achieved, and an optimal time frame for this overload to occur. A gradual and systematic increase of the workload over a period of time will result in improvements in fitness without risk of injury. If overload occurs too slowly, improvement is unlikely, but overload that is increased too rapidly may result in injury or muscle damage. For example, the athlete who exercises vigorously only on weekends violates the principle of progression and most likely will not see obvious fitness gains.

The principle of progression also stresses the need for proper rest and recovery. Continual stress on the body and constant overload will result in exhaustion and injury. Rest should be incorporated into every workout plan in order to prevent overtraining, injury, and decreased fitness.

The applications to our strivings to become More Fit 4 the Kingdom of God can be readily seen here. President Hinckley often gave charges such as these:

"...far more of us need to awake and arouse our faculties to an awareness of the great everlasting truths of the gospel of Jesus Christ. Each of us can do a little better than we have been doing. We can be a little more kind. We can be a little more merciful. We can be a little more forgiving. We can put behind us our weaknesses of the past, and go forth with new energy and increased resolution to improve the world about us, in our homes, in our places of employment, in our social activities... We have work to do, you and I, so very much of it. Let us roll up our sleeves and get at it, with a new commitment, putting our trust in the Lord" (Hinckley, 1995).

APPLICATION & DISCUSSION | CH 4 | 1.1
Consider how you can "be a little more" for answering the following questions:

1. *Which of these "we can be a little more" statements resonate with you as a way you want to improve? How do you think that will be impactful in your life to do so?*

   _____

   _____

   _____

   _____

2. *What about as a family? Which "we can be a little more" statements seem to fit a family need for improvement?*

   _____

   _____

   _____

   _____

(For a blank copy of this "Application & Discussion" see the Appendix)

Yet, those strivings to be a "little better" should be just that – little, steady, incremental, steps. Fitness programs – whether they be intellectual, physical, spiritual, or social – that add too much too quick, result in injury or failure, both of which put an end to progression. If not careful, we can easily become discouraged with self-improvement efforts and the seemingly never-ending list of things to work on. In despair, we then conclude, "I can't do all these things!" or "I will never be as good as all these people!" Addressing these concerns, Elder Cornish pleaded that members must stop comparing themselves to others. He said, "We torture ourselves needlessly by competing and comparing. We falsely judge our self-worth by the things we do or don't have and by the opinions of others" (Cornish, 2016). He then perfectly taught the importance of measuring performance. "If we must compare," said he, "let us compare how we were in the past to how we are today—and even to how we want to be in the future" (Cornish, 2016).

Thus, while we should be "anxiously engaged in a good cause" we also must do all things "in wisdom and order" and not "run faster than we have strength" (D&C 58:26-27, Mosiah 4:27). Elder Ballard summarized this important balance:

> "{Accepting] and living the gospel of Christ can be challenging. It has always been thus, and it ever will be. Life can be like hikers ascending a steep and arduous trail. It is a natural and normal thing to occasionally pause on the path to catch our breath, to recalculate our bearings, and to reconsider our pace. Not everyone needs to pause on the path, but there is nothing wrong with doing so when your circumstances require. In fact, it can be a positive thing for those who take full advantage of the opportunity to refresh themselves with the living water of the gospel of Christ...The danger comes when someone chooses to wander away from the path that leads to the tree of

life. Sometimes we can learn, study, and know, and sometimes we have to believe, trust, and hope" (Ballard, 2016).

APPLICATION & DISCUSSION | CH 4 | 1.2
Consider what it means to take a "productive pause."

1. *What are some ways you've found to take a "productive pause" as you strive to progress?*

_____

_____

_____

_____

2. *What does that look like and how have you found it helpful?*

_____

_____

_____

_____

(For a blank copy of this "Application & Discussion" see the Appendix)

Adaptation

Adaptation refers to the body's ability to adjust to increased or decreased physical demands. It is also a way one learns to coordinate muscle movement and develop sports-specific skills, such as batting, swimming freestyle, or shooting free throws. Repeatedly practicing a skill or activity makes it "second-nature" and easier to perform. Adaptation explains why beginning exercisers are often sore after starting a new routine, but after doing the same exercise for a few weeks they have little, if any, muscle soreness.

Additionally, adaptation makes an athlete very efficient. Efficiency then allows him to expend less energy doing the same movements. Having adapted to the ability of more efficiently performing a workout routine, the athlete needs to vary the workout to see continued improvement.

This principle of adaptation also has its correlation in becoming more spiritually fit. On the positive side, President Heber J. Grant often shared a saying attributed to Ralph Waldo Emerson, "That which we persist in doing becomes easier for us to do—not that the nature of the thing is changed, but that our power to do is increased" (Grant, 2011). In becoming more fit spiritually, there are many exercises that it would be good to do repeatedly. Such exercises include prayer, scripture study, temple attendance, and partaking of the sacrament, to name a few. Socially we could include things like expressing gratitude, volunteering, and writing thank you cards. You get the idea. Choosing to engage in activities such as these can be difficult at first, but as we develop the habit, they become much easier to incorporate consistently.

Thus, it's not so much that we do things *repeatedly* that is a problem, it's when we do things *mindlessly*. Our spirits, minds, and bodies need to be challenged in order to adapt and get stronger. If we do three sets of 10 push-ups every day for a year, we will become really good at doing 3 sets of 10 push-ups… and nothing more. We need to regularly increase the difficulty and/or variety of our workouts in order to get different results. This type of adaptation is different than that spoken of by President Grant and could be aptly described as "going through the motions."

This version of adaptation was elaborated upon by President Uchtdorf. He asked:

"When our time in mortality is complete, what experiences will we be able to share about our own contribution to this significant period of our lives and to the furthering of the Lord's work? Will we be able to say that we rolled up our sleeves and labored with all our heart, might, mind, and strength? Or will we have to admit that our role was mostly that of an observer?" (Uchtdorf, 2014).

President Uchtdorf suggested that there are three reasons that contribute to becoming "a bit sleepy" in regard to striving to become More Fit 4 the Kingdom: Selfishness, Addictions, and Competing Priorities (Uchtdorf, 2014).

Summary

Just as an athlete might need to add a little more weight, a slightly steeper incline, or a few more minutes of training in order to sustain continual strength and fitness gains, so must we as individuals and families as we seek to improve our overall fitness. "I will give unto the children of men line upon line, precept upon precept, here a little and there a little," said the Lord (2 Ne 28:30). Indeed, His training model *is* the overload principle: "[Blessed] are those who hearken unto my precepts, and lend an ear unto my counsel, for they shall learn wisdom; for unto him that receiveth I will give more..." (2 Ne 28:30).

The Lord isn't expecting us to be perfect. That's impossible. Rather, He invites us to be (or become) worthy, and ultimately to become perfected in Him (Moro. 10:32). He wants more than anything else to have all of His children come back home to live with Him as families forever. This effort at a balanced, consistent - albeit imperfect effort - was summarized well by President Hinckley, who on several occasions said, "Just do the best you can, but be sure it is your very best" (Hinckley, 2004). "Doing the best you can" – or applying the overload principle – means recognizing where we need to improve, and then carefully trying to make the improvement, little by little. By engaging in this process, the Holy Ghost will help us know what adjustments to make in order become more aligned with our covenants.

APPLICATION & DISCUSSION | CH 4 | 1.3

Consider how we try to identify areas to improve in and still remain positive:

1. *What are some truths you've learned that help identify weaknesses but not become weakened in the process?*

    _____

    _____

    _____

    _____

    _____

    _____

    _____

    _____

    _____

    _____

(For a blank copy of this "Application & Discussion" see the Appendix)

THE OVERLOAD PRINCIPLE | *core concepts*

- Like Milo of Croton, the best way to gain strength is by following a program of progressive resistance for an extended period of time.

- Sometimes we mistakenly believe that happiness is the absence of a load. Bearing a load is a necessary and essential part of the plan of happiness.

- Small efforts sustained over time can produce significant results.

- Any kind of fitness program that adds too much too quick, will likely result in injury or failure - both of which put an end to progression. If not careful, we can become discouraged with self-improvement efforts and the seemingly never-ending list of things to work on.

- Adaptation can be good... "That which we persist in doing becomes easier for us to do—not that the nature of the thing is changed, but that our power to do is increased"

- Adaptation can be bad... It's not so much that we do things *repeatedly* that is a problem, it's when we do things *mindlessly*. Our spirits, minds, and bodies need to be challenged in order to adapt and get stronger.

- "Doing our best" means that we recognize where we need to improve, and then carefully try to make the improvement, little by little. That is the overload principle.

Chapter 5
OVERCOMING PLATEAUS

Michael Phelps was in trouble. He was seventh out of eight swimmers midway through the 100-meter butterfly of the 2008 Summer Olympics in Beijing. His quest to tie, let alone surpass, Mark Spitz's record of seven golds in one Olympics was in jeopardy. This was the sixth event on his schedule, the 100-meter butterfly, and was the one experts thought might trip him up. It was his only individual race of less than 200 meters. It was also the only individual event he entered here in which he didn't already hold the world record. Even more pressing, he'd have to pass 6 swimmers in the next 50 meters in order to win.

With less than 15 meters to go, Phelps had made remarkable progress. Known for his astounding stamina, he'd managed to maintain the pace of his first 50 meters, passing 5 other swimmers as they tapered off. Still, Serbia's Milorad Cavic, who held the lead at the turn, seemed to have an insurmountable lead. Phelps then made a critical decision. Going completely against his training, Phelps attempted another half-stroke. Instead of gliding into the wall as Cavic had chosen, Phelps hoped to somehow out-touch the Serbian.

His hands came down through the water and touched the wall .01 seconds before Cavic finished his glide to the wall! No one could believe it. Not the roaring crowd at the National Aquatics Center. Not the swimmers in the pool. Not the millions of fans who were glued to their TVs watching the frame-by-frame replays being shown worldwide. Not even Phelps. "I had to take my goggles off first to make sure the '1' was next to my name," he said (Svrluga, 2008).

Phelps's time of 50.58 seconds was a new Olympic record. His margin of victory was literally by a fingernail. He beat Cavic by .01 of a second. Serbian swimming officials filed a protest and who could blame them? But the results confirmed what no one could believe; Michael Phelps had won! What made the difference? Phelps told us the secret:

> "When I did chop the last stroke, I really thought that cost me the race. But it happened to be the direct opposite. If I would've glided, I would've ended up being way too long. I ended up making the right decision" (Svrluga, 2008).

Phelps chose to increase the frequency of his stroke, one of the three main factors to adjust in order to break out of a plateau. His choice to do so won him a gold in one of the most memorable and unbelievable Olympic events of all-time.

Adjusting the Variables

While it's very unlikely any of us will be in the water on the world's biggest stage when we're faced with the choice to break out of a plateau, we will all encounter the experience of "leveling off," or "hitting a wall." With physical fitness plans this usually occurs 3-6 months into a new training program. The dramatic gains we saw initially seem to dry up. In order to avoid this, physical training plans require constant adjustment. In Michael Phelps's case, all he needed was a half stroke. The same may be true in our efforts to become more spiritually fit. At some point, we'll all need a small change in our routine.

As outlined in chapter 4, "The Overload Principle," initial training must exceed the typical daily demand. For example, a weightlifter gradually adds weight to a barbell to build strength. Endurance athletes increase training time and intensity to improve race performances, etc. The overload stimulates changes designed to help the body cope with the growing demands on the muscles and other systems. Once the body has adapted, however, a different stimulus is required to continue the change. To continue making gains, one of these three variables needs to be manipulated: duration, frequency, or intensity.

To help describe the application of these variables in the realm of physical fitness, I'll use a distance runner as an example. Let's say a distance runner has progressed to the point where they're running 5 days a week for 24 minutes and can run 3 miles in that time period. While initially excited about the 8-minute mile pace, they've grown frustrated after several weeks of little to no improvement. They're confused; "Why have my gains ceased?!" They've followed the same training regimen that enabled them to make the gains that brought them to the point they're at – what's happened?

Adjusting the Variables: Physically

One possible answer is that the distance runner has maxed out their individual capacity. There's a point of diminishing returns in terms of fitness gains; there's only so fast a human being can run, right? However, while impressive, an 8-minute mile pace is likely not their top speed. Chances are, the distance runner could overcome this plateau and improve their time. Their body has simply adapted to their exercise routine. It brought gains at first, but now they're only able to maintain their running time. The runner has a few options and they all involve adjusting one or more of the following variables; duration, frequency, and intensity. Let's look at all three:

- Duration: They could maintain the same frequency of runs (5 days a week), and also the same intensity (8-minute miles), but try to run 4 miles at each workout, instead of 3.

- Frequency: They could maintain the same duration and intensity (24-minute 3-mile splits) but increase the frequency from 5 days a week to 6.

- Intensity: They could maintain both the duration and frequency of their runs (24-minute runs 5 days a week) but attempt to run a greater distance within that time, like 3.25 miles rather than 3.

Of course, to accelerate the process, the runner could attempt to make changes to all of the variables simultaneously. They could start running 4 miles, 6 days a week, within a 30-minute period. Such an approach should be taken cautiously, however. Too much change, too quick, can lead to injury. Normally, the manipulation of just one variable at a time is all that's needed to break out of a plateau. Once that's done, the distance runner, or any other athlete, will start making gains again!

Spiritual Plateaus

Athletes aren't the only ones who fall into plateaus. Professionals in every field feel this at times, as do students at every level of education, parents, families, church leaders, etc. They happen for the same reasons. Let's take spiritual plateaus, for example. Having experienced seasons of dramatic gains as a full-time missionary, a challenging new calling at church, a week-long summer camp experience, we find that our "gains" have leveled off and that we are in a state of little or no change or closeness to God. The same holds true for families; after gaining so much closeness on a family vacation or having had a good run of several months of FHE suddenly we find our progress slowing or coming to a halt altogether. Like Milorad Cavic in the 100-meter butterfly, we find ourselves "gliding" to the finish. Even when unintentional, if left unchecked these glides, or "spiritual plateaus," can turn into full-blown complacency. Elder Maxwell described this when he taught:

> "Happily, many of us have already picked and been greatly nourished by the low-hanging fruit from the gospel tree. Yet, on the higher branches, much fruit still remains, unreached for and unplucked... The higher hanging fruits also embody the sweet savor of submissiveness, the nourishing nectar of consecration, and the milk of meekness" (Maxwell, 2003).

This "higher hanging" fruit awaits our stretching grasp, and the effort to reach them isn't an obstruction to our happiness, but a purposeful manifestation of God's intent to love and strengthen us as we reach, or like in the example of Michael Phelps, as we take the extra "half stroke" (See also 1 Nephi 8:10-11; 11:7,21-22). Just as in physical fitness, as we seek to become More Fit 4 the Kingdom, we need to adjust or "stretch" the variables of our "training programs."

Filling Our Spiritual Tanks

This process reminds me of many of the courageous people I've had the privilege of working with. In chapter 1, I shared a story about "John and Sally," a couple experiencing marital difficulty. Like that story, the following is also a composite of multiple experiences I've had as a Bishop. For convenience, I'll refer to the individual in this story as "Sally" as well.

Sally set up an appointment to meet with me. She was worn out. She felt defeated, deflated, and depressed. The stress and busyness of life had become unbearable and there seemed to be no end in sight. She wanted to keep on going, she wanted to keep it up, but she just didn't feel like she could do it all anymore. She was ready to give up.

Like so many, Sally was giving valiant and tireless efforts to her marriage and children, to managing her home, and to serving in the Church and community. However, she'd given very little time to herself.

In response to inquiries about taking time for herself to go on dates with her spouse, on outings with friends, or even shopping for herself, she said that she just didn't have time for that sort that thing. She gave me a similar response when I asked her about temple attendance, personal scripture study, and personal prayer routines. As we talked, I sensed that while she believed all these personal endeavors were worthwhile, she also felt that in some way they were a little "selfish." As such, she wasn't making time for them because her marriage and kids needed her time more than she did.

While concurring that the other things she was spending her time with with were important and needed to be attended to, I expressed to Sally my concern that her "spiritual tank" was running low. I counseled her to consider making more time for herself in these areas and assured her they weren't selfish endeavors. I encouraged her to consider them as necessary aid to help gain the spiritual and emotional energy required to press on with the strength to carry the load she was pulling.

At a time in her life where she needed more spiritual strength, more comfort, and more reassurance from the Lord than ever, she wasn't letting Him provide it (Alma 37:6-7). As a result of her unintentional self-neglect, she'd plateaued spiritually and emotionally. She was on the brink physically, as well. She was following the admonition of King Benjamin - to be diligent - but had disregarded his counsel to not "run faster than [she] had strength" (Mosiah 4:27).

Accordingly, our efforts together soon centered around getting her the "spiritual fuel" she needed. Our work consisted of logistically figuring out how she could incorporate these important exercises into her busy life and in helping her feel spiritually justified in doing so. The later part proved the hardest. However, as we studied the scriptures and words of the prophets, Sally came to understand that these weren't selfish efforts after all but were endeavors essential to her spiritual well-being. In essence, we worked to implement the teachings President Harold B. Lee offered so many years ago: "You cannot lift another soul until you are standing on higher ground than he is. You cannot light a fire in another soul unless it is burning in your own soul" (Lee, 1973).

Sufficient Spiritual Strength

At times, we all find ourselves in a position similar to Sally. As individuals and families, we are in need of spiritual strength and increased understanding of how to overcome the spiritual plateaus we find ourselves in. While we might be able to move forward for a season due to the momentum of our past "strokes," what propelled us in the past won't propel us indefinitely into the future. We need to keep taking strokes. Elder Eying taught:

> "The spiritual strength sufficient for our youth to stand firm just a few years ago will soon not be enough. Many of them are remarkable in their spiritual maturity and in their faith. But even the best of them are sorely tested. And the testing will become more severe" (Eyring, 2001).

Notice some of the key implications of his statement and how they related to the principles of plateauing:

1. *The duration, frequency, and intensity with which they ran a few years ago was good, but insufficient now.*

2. *The contest they are involved in today, is much more competitive than it was in the past.*

Compare this to the statement Elder Ballard made the following year:

"These are 'perilous times.' We battle literally for the souls of men. The enemy is unforgiving and relentless. He is taking eternal prisoners at an alarming rate. And he shows no sign of letting up…While we are profoundly grateful for the many members of the Church who are doing great things in the battle for truth and right, I must honestly tell you it still is not enough. We need much more help" (Ballard, 2002).

Now is the Time to Get Fueled Up

The message is clear: Now is the time to be strong. Now is the time to break out of a plateau and move forward. Now is the time to make sure we are keeping our spiritual tanks full. To help guide us all as we seek to receive the spiritual strength the Lord has promised to make available, the following exercises have been outlined in the *For the Strength of Youth* pamphlet – Exercises:

1. *Kneel each morning and night in prayer to your Father in Heaven.*
2. *Study the scriptures each day and apply what you read to your life.*
3. *Strive each day to be obedient and make and keep covenants.*
4. *Attend the temple and feel the joy and peace that come from serving in the house of the Lord.*
5. *Young men commit to serve a full-time mission.*
6. *Follow the teachings of the prophets, the other authorities of the Church, and your local leaders. They will lead you in paths of happiness.*
7. *Be humble and willing to listen to the Holy Ghost and respond to His promptings. Place the wisdom of the Lord above your own wisdom (Church 2011).*

As we do these things, we are promised the following strength – Promises:

1. *The Lord will make much more out of your life than you can by yourself.*
2. *He will increase your opportunities, expand your vision, and strengthen you.*
3. *He will give you the help you need to meet your trials and challenges.*
4. *You will gain a stronger testimony and find true joy as you come to know your Father in Heaven and His Son, Jesus Christ, and feel Their love for you (Church 2011).*

APPLICATION & DISCUSSION | CH 5 | 1.0
Consider how the exercises and promises above have or could impact you and your family:

1. *Identify 1-2 of the exercises above that you're already doing well:*

_____

_____

_____

_____

2. *Identify 1-2 of the exercises above you want to improve in:*

_____

_____

_____

_____

3. *Identify a promise that you most sincerely want to secure:*

_____

_____

_____

(For a blank copy of this "Application & Discussion" see the Appendix)

Adjusting the Variables: Spiritually

Knowing some of the key exercises required to become More Fit 4 the Kingdom, and the promises available for doing so, if we have found ourselves plateaued in any of these areas, the process of breaking through them is the same as it is physically: adjust the variables of duration, frequency, and intensity. An example of this process applied spiritually comes from the teachings of Elder Bednar. While not as straight forward as in the example of the runner, notice how the principles of duration, frequency, and intensity are incorporated into his instruction on how to "pray always:"

> "There may be things in our character, in our behavior, or concerning our spiritual growth about which we need to counsel with Heavenly Father in morning prayer. After expressing appropriate thanks for blessings received, we plead for understanding, direction, and help to do the things we cannot do in our own strength alone...

> "Such a prayer is a key part of the spiritual preparation for our day.

> "During the course of the day, we keep a prayer in our heart for continued assistance and guidance—even as Alma suggested: 'Let all thy thoughts be directed unto the Lord' (Alma 37:36).

> "We notice during this particular day that there are occasions where normally we would have a tendency to speak harshly, and we do not; or we might be inclined to anger, but we are not. We discern heavenly

help and strength and humbly recognize answers to our prayer. Even in that moment of recognition, we offer a silent prayer of gratitude.

"At the end of our day, we kneel again and report back to our Father. We review the events of the day and express heartfelt thanks for the blessings and the help we received. We repent and, with the assistance of the Spirit of the Lord, identify ways we can do and become better tomorrow. Thus, our evening prayer builds upon and is a continuation of our morning prayer. And our evening prayer also is a preparation for meaningful morning prayer.

"Morning and evening prayers—and all of the prayers in between—are not unrelated, discrete events; rather, they are linked together each day and across days, weeks, months, and even years. This is in part how we fulfill the scriptural admonition to 'pray always' (Luke 21:36; 3 Nephi 18:15, 18; D&C 31:12). Such meaningful prayers are instrumental in obtaining the highest blessings God holds in store for His faithful children" (Bednar, 2008).

Using Elder Bednar's teachings as a template, we can see multiple ways to break out of a spiritual plateau in prayer. For example, let's say a person is praying 5 days a week, morning and night, for about 2 minutes each time they pray. As they pray, they regularly express gratitude for key elements of their day and life, and occasionally ask for divine assistance to help them in some of the challenges they face. They've been consistent, but they feel like they're "going through the motions." What do they do?

- *Duration: They could choose to maintain the same frequency of prayer (5 days a week), and also the same intensity (praying for the same sort of things in regard to gratitude and assistance), but try to pray for 5 minutes each attempt, instead of 2, and as Elder Bednar suggested, keep their morning and evening prayers "linked together."*

- *Frequency: They could maintain the same duration and intensity (2-minute prayers offering gratitude and asking for assistance), but could increase the frequency of their prayers, not just from 5 days a week to 7, but also by offering multiple, less formal prayers throughout each day.*

- *Intensity: They could maintain both the duration and frequency of their prayers (2-minute offerings, 5 days a week), but could increase their intensity by recognizing strength and assistance they received throughout the day or writing down the questions they're asking during each prayer. This process would enable them to review their "prayer pattern" and note pleas that are repeated and others that are no longer as important.*

Like the distance runner, the individual attempting to break out of their prayer plateau could also make changes to all of the variables; praying on their knees vocally 5 minutes, twice a day, 7 days a week, linking their prayers together throughout the day, recognizing and recording divine assistance and revelation as it comes. Of course, the same caution would apply – too much change too soon could lead to "injury." In the spiritual sense, this would most likely be a feeling of being overwhelmed. Thus, a careful approach should be considered. Whatever variable or combination of variables is adjusted, the result will be the same: a breakout of the spiritual plateau caused by the comfort of an old regimen and the beginning of new spiritual gains.

Summary

While there's plenty of evidence that the individuals and families of the Church today are among the very best the Church has ever had, this is not the time for us to plateau, become complacent, or try to do it all on our own. President Monson taught that, "We live in perilous times; the signs are all around us...We, as members of The Church of Jesus Christ of Latter-day Saints, must stand up to the dangers which surround us and our families" (Monson, 2005).

The path to eternal life is an incline, not on a plateau. The path leads onward, and upward. "Hence, ever-increasing spiritual understanding and energy are required to reach our destination" (Hilbig, 2007). The devil will try to convince us otherwise. From the Book of Mormon we read, "At that day shall [the devil] … lull them away into carnal security, that they will say: All is well in Zion; yea, Zion prospereth, all is well—and thus the devil cheateth their souls" (2 Nephi 28:20-21). But as we identify personal plateaus and break free by adjusting the duration, frequency, or intensity of our actions, we will engage in sustained spiritual growth toward our desired destination.

APPLICATION & DISCUSSION: CHAPTER 5 | 1.1
See "Overcoming Plateaus" at the end of this chapter for an individual example of how to adjust the variables in the 4 areas of total fitness. Then make a copy of a blank copy of "Overcoming Plateaus" from the Appendix and develop your own plan to break out of a plateau. Perhaps there will be some crossover with the MOREFIT goals you set on "Application & Discussion: Chapter 2 | 1.0 | the MOREFIT goal setting & achieving strategy;" maybe there won't. Either way, evaluate and see how you could utilize this tool as an individual or as a family. Remember, in most cases, only one variable needs to be adjusted at a time to start seeing gains again.

OVERCOMING PLATEAUS | *core concepts*

- By making a single change to a single variable, his stroke frequency, Michael Phelps broke out of a plateau. His choice won him a gold medal.

- When our spirits, minds, or bodies adapt, a different stimulus is required to continue making positive change and improvement. A manipulation to one of these three variables will create that stimulus: duration, frequency, or intensity.

- Even when unintentional, spiritual glides or plateaus, can turn to full-blown complacency.

- While me might be able to move forward for a season due to the momentum of our past "strokes," what propelled us forward in the past won't propel us indefinitely into the future. We need to keep taking strokes!

- Now is the time to be strong. Now is the time to break out of a plateau and move forward. Now is the time to make sure we our keeping our spiritual tanks full.

- We need to be careful not to make too much change too soon. That can lead to "injury," or in the spiritual sense, to the feeling of being "overwhelmed."

- The path to eternal life is on an incline, not a plateau. The path leads onward, and upward. Thus, we will need ever-increasing spiritual understanding and energy to reach our destination.

DISCUSSION & APPLICATION: CHAPTER 5 | 1.1 (individual)			
Overcoming Plateaus			
THE 4 AREAS OF FITNESS	DURATION: The length of time spent doing the exercise	FREQUENCY: The number of times each week or month	INTENSITY: The level of focus or specificity
WISDOM INTELLECTUAL EXERCISE: **Homework**	I'm currently spending 2 hours a day... not much to change there	I'm already doing it every day... unfortunately.	I need to focus more during my 2 hours! Only look at my phone after 50 minutes of study.
STATURE PHYSICAL EXERCISE: **Jogging**	I've been running for 30 minutes. I'm going to get up earlier and increase that to 45 minutes!!	I'm doing it Mon-Fri. I'm going to leave it the same. I need my Sat's for sleep	I'm going to maintain my pace for now (9min mile) but that's what I'll adjust next!
FAVOR WITH GOD SPIRITUAL EXERCISE: **Prayer**	When I pray it's good, but the key word there is "when"	I'm going to make it a rule to pray when I come back from my run in the morning and before I go to bed at night!	I also want to increase my intensity by kneeling and praying vocally.
FAVOR WITH MAN SOCIAL EXERCISE: **Getting Along With Family**	I haven't been making any time for my siblings... at all. So, I'm going to plan 5 minutes with one each daily	I'm going to TRY «to spend 5 mims 5 days a week. I'm giving myself a couple days as a buffer... I need my space!	I'm just going to be as interested and kind to them as is possible for me to be...

DISCUSSION & APPLICATION: CHAPTER 5	1.1 (family)		
Overcoming Plateaus			
THE 4 AREAS OF FITNESS	DURATION: The length of time spent doing the exercise	FREQUENCY: The number of times each week or month	INTENSITY: The level of focus or specificity
WISDOM INTELLECTUAL EXERCISE: **Help with Homework**	As parents, and older siblings, we can make ourselves more available during homework time. When the kids are working on it and we're home, we're all theirs!	We will do this whenever we're home. There will be days we can't, but we will prioritize "parent tutor time" to help the kids feel supported	Hopefully we can help... Most of the things these kids study I can't remember!
STATURE PHYSICAL EXERCISE: **Hug More Often**	This might be more of a "social" goal but we need to do it! A hug doesn't last long and we aren't giving enough of them	We'd like to make it a rule to hug one another when we leave in the morning. A quick hug and an "I love you!" goes a long way for everyone	At times we will have to just "grin and bear it" but we think if we sincerely hug one another we can really impact our togetherness
FAVOR WITH GOD SPIRITUAL EXERCISE: **Temple Attendance with our Teens**	Depending on when we go, it's usually about 60-90 minutes, plus travel	We need to set a date, take the kids out of school, get to the temple, and to lunch. It will ensure it happens and that it's a looked forward to event!	The temple provides all the "intensity" we need!
FAVOR WITH MAN SOCIAL EXERCISE: **Discussions at Dinner Time**	We eat together just about every night; not much we can do to change or improve that	We have conversation all the time, and good ones. They just happen spontaneously	We will try to more deliberately use the time to discuss various challenging scenarios that might come up: "What would you do if _____"

Chapter 6

RUN YOUR OWN RACE

Too often as members of the Church, we let our spiritual self-esteem sink far beneath what it could be. Comments such as, "I am just not good enough," "I fall so far short," and "I will never measure up" characterize the feelings of too many youth and adults. Elder Holland commented on this, quoting Sister Darla Isackson, saying, "Satan has somehow managed to make covenants and commandments seem like curses and condemnations. For some he has turned the ideals and inspiration of the gospel into self-loathing and misery-making" (Holland, 2017).

Consequently, too many of us go for long periods of time missing out or falling short of, the purpose of life that Lehi described, to "have joy" (2 Nephi 2:25). We belittle and beat ourselves up, feeling we don't nor ever will "measure up." One might even argue that a book entitled *More Fit 4 the Kingdom* sounds just like one more way to fall short! But such is just the opposite. All who have a willingness to repent (change and improve) and a desire to become more righteous (more spiritually fit) can find joy in the process of becoming More Fit 4 the Kingdom.

Repenting & Repairing are Part of the Plan

Concerning the low spiritual self-esteem many members have, Elder Cornish provided some great insight. In response to the aforementioned questions, "Am I good enough?" and "Will I make it?," he stated very succinctly: "'Yes! You are going to be good enough' and 'Yes, you are going to make it as long as you keep repenting and do not rationalize or rebel.'" Inserting some concepts from this book synonymous this promise, it reads as follows: "'Yes! You are going to be good enough' and 'Yes, you are going to make it as long as you keep *changing through progressive overload* and don't *quit* or *plateau.*'"

We all need to keep in mind that Heavenly Father is a loving Father. It is his work and glory that we return to live with Him, as families, forever (Moses 1:39). Indeed - He's rooting for us to succeed! President J. Reuben Clark, Jr., testified similarly:

> "You know, I believe that the Lord will help us. I believe if we go to him, he will give us wisdom, if we are living righteously. I believe he will answer our prayers. I believe that our Heavenly Father wants to save every one of his children. I do not think he intends to shut any of us off because of some slight transgression, some slight failure to observe some rule or regulation. There are the great elementals that we must observe, but he is not going to be captious (tending to find fault or raise petty objections) about the lesser things... I believe that his juridical concept of

his dealings with his children could be expressed in this way: I believe that in his justice and mercy, he will give us the maximum reward for our acts, give us all that he can give, and in the reverse, I believe that he will impose upon us the minimum penalty which it is possible for him to impose" (Clark, 1953).

Therefore, we should take confidence in knowing that as we strive to become More Fit 4 the Kingdom, repenting and repairing is part of the plan – not a violation of it. Elder Holland added, "I would hope we could pursue personal improvement in a way that doesn't include getting ulcers or anorexia, feeling depressed or demolishing our self-esteem" (Holland, 2017).

Learning from the Lessons

This book has highlighted athletic champions whose endeavors embody many of the core principles of becoming More Fit 4 the Kingdom. From Tiger Woods we learned the importance of having the courage to change and improve in positive ways, that our ability to maximize performance and productivity depend on it. From Michael Jordan we learned that failure should be both accepted and expected. By creating plans to overcome our weaknesses once they've been exposed, we can harness the power that awareness affords us. From Diana Nyad we learned that while we'll have many obstacles along our path and many failed attempts along our way, the data gleaned from facing those obstacles and failures can become the reason for our success in the future. By learning to track, measure, and define success appropriately we can "find a way" to accomplish our goals. From Milo of Croton we learned that we can gain impressive levels of strength by following a program of progressive resistance, adding a little to our load over an extended period of time. As a result, we can improve our overall fitness to levels previously thought unattainable. And finally, from Michael Phelps we learned that by making small adjustments to our regular routines we can break out of plateaus and put ourselves back on a path of experiencing new growth and new gains.

However, the example from this book that perhaps best exemplifies the process of becoming More Fit 4 the Kingdom, is that of Lindsey Jacobellis. You'll remember her crash in the Olympics was highlighted in the introduction to illustrate the importance of keeping our guard up. Lindsey had let hers down and had it cost her an opportunity that she may never get back again. While what she chose to do in that particular race cost her an Olympic gold, she has since chosen not to let that moment defeat or define her. Instead, she not only got back on the course during that race, but she's continued to race till this day.

While yet to win that elusive Olympic gold, Lindsey's resilient spirit hasn't allowed her to abandon the quest. Having qualified for the Olympics three times since 2006, she appears to be undaunted by her infamous fall. Still, luck has yet to turn her way. In 2010, she was disqualified in Vancouver after hitting a gate. In 2014, she fell in Sochi. And in 2018, she made it back to the medal round and led most of the way only to be passed by several riders in the late stages and ended up finishing in 4th place, 3 hundredths (.03) of a second behind the 3rd place finisher.

How then does Lindsey best exemplify the process of becoming More Fit 4 the Kingdom? The other champions all overcame their obstacles and came out on top – aren't they better examples? Not necessarily. The race of life isn't about "winning" in the way we traditionally think of it. It's about trying, failing, strategizing, strengthening, changing, improving, then trying and sometimes failing again. It's not so much a matter of whether we'll crash or go off course, as much as it's about whether we'll choose to continue to reach for the Savior when we do. As Nephi taught, "[Ye] have not come this far save it were by the word of Christ with unshaken faith in him, relying wholly upon the merits of him who is mighty to save. Wherefore, ye must press forward with a steadfastness in Christ..." (2 Nephi 31:19-20). Like Lindsey, we all just need to keep getting back up and strive to give it our best.

Run Your Own Race

"Run your own race!" This is the type of thing runners say before an event, kind of a "sermon in a sentence." It can mean a lot of things. For example, it can mean, "have a clear vision for your race plan," or "look toward your own goals." It can also mean, "don't focus too much on who's next to you or who's behind you, but focus on beating your own best time." Whether you're actually running a race, trying to improve your grades in school, growing closer to God, or hoping to strengthen a relationship, the concept of learning to "run your own race" is an important one to understand. Let me emphasize the concept by utilizing the example of a marathon runner and compare their effort with our own quest to become More Fit 4 the Kingdom. Let's start with some similarities:

First, in a marathon, it does us no good to sprint out ahead only to crash, fade, or go off course moments later. You'll see this happen a lot at elementary school jog-a-thons; many of the kids get so excited about the starting gun and the cheering fans that they run as fast as they can their first lap or two, only to realize they can't maintain that pace. They end up walking the rest of the laps, while their wiser classmates who chose to run at a more realistic pace continue to circle them on the track.

In all my races, I've felt the same temptation at the start – "Let's go! Just let your body run!" I've even felt a competitive voice saying, "You can keep up with *that* guy!" or "You can't let *that* runner beat you!" But as I've kept in my mind to "run my race" and that my goal is completing, not competing with anyone other than myself, I've been able to maintain a strong pace and finish the races I've entered. Life is the same way; it's a marathon, not a sprint. It requires a good start and a consistent effort all the way to the finish.

Second, effective marathon runners set goals. They've got goals for race day and goals for their training. My goal for each race has been created as the result of the months of running data I've accumulated. I've analyzed my runs and chosen a pace and finish time that would be challenging but attainable. Nevertheless, despite my careful planning, each race has thrown variables that have caused me to adjust.

During one of my races, I felt great from the start, but my wife felt sick and mentally fatigued early on. My goal quickly changed from "Let's set a PR!" to "Let's get Jacque to the finish!" Looking back, while I didn't reach the goal-time I had set out to achieve, that race is easily my most "successful" run. Jacque and I both completed the race, crossing the finish line together at the same exact second! This pattern of adjustment and adaptation has been a part of all my races. Having goals and plans are essential components of race day success, but you always need to be ready to make adjustments – even some concessions – along the way. Success in the race of life comes the same way; we set goals (preferably

MOREFIT goals), keep them constantly before our eyes, regularly review our progress, and frequently revise them as circumstances dictate.

Third, "Success results when preparation meets opportunity" (Wirthlin, 1989). Marathon runners get this, and those in the race of life should, too. They didn't just wake up, go outside, and run 26.2 miles the first day they decided to get involved in the sport. They train regularly, slowly building the skill, strength, and stamina required, and when the race day comes, they're prepared to perform.

For me, I knew that logging the requisite miles was crucial, but realized early on that if I didn't plan ahead in a practical way, the miles would never be run. These practical measures included simple things like setting my alarm clock, laying out my clothes the night before, having my nutrition and hydration already measured out and ready to go, and knowing exactly what route I'd run. Doing these simple things helped me be ready for the morning runs when they arrived, and my bed was begging me, "Crawl back inside!" Likewise, while we may not be able to control when our "race day" opportunities will come in life, we can count on the opportunities coming at some point and make practical preparations to be well prepared for when they do.

Fourth, marathon runners rely upon trusted friends, experts, and coaches for help. Ahead of the marathon, they plan workouts, meals, and sleeping patterns based on their advice. Come race day, they feed off the strength of their fans and loved ones. They take advantage of watching others compete, learning from their strengths and weaknesses, and also identifying difficult stretches on the course. Additionally, they hit up aid stations along the way, getting nutrition, hydration, and - if necessary - medical attention.

I've been fortunate in all the races I've run to have family and friends meet me along the route. They've been there with signs and support, high fives and hugs. It's hard to explain, but they've given me a tangible boost of strength and energy and a desire to keep moving forward that wouldn't have come without them. We need to emulate that reliance on others in our race of life. Part of being truly "self-reliant" is learning that we've never done all we can until we've sought help from the Lord and our loved ones. Simply put, we can't do it without them, especially Him.

Fifth and finally, effective runners stay on course. While the course, weather, physical fatigue, and mental strain stand as foes attempting to push them off track, marathon runners have learned to trust their training. The mental toughness they've gained from months of getting up in the early hours and enduring grueling, monotonous, and seemingly endless runs helps enable them to endure.

During our first attempt at a marathon, my wife got injured just weeks out from the event. Having come as far as I had, I chose to stay signed up for the race and see what I could do. Things were going great up to about mile 22 or 23 when all around me it seemed like runners were dropping out. One runner simply stopped and walked off the course. I could see her trailing off in the distance, with seemingly no desire to finish the last few miles. Another runner, having been very strong throughout, literally crashed to the ground less than a quarter mile in front of me. Medical professionals rushed to his aid, but severe muscle cramps rendered him unable to finish. Doing fine up to this point, these tragedies began to weigh on my mind. However, the thought of meeting my wife at the finish line helped me muster the strength needed to press on. Likewise, in order to successfully run the course of life, so must we. The righteous way of life, the straight and narrow path, is the only course that leads to happiness, joy, and peace (see 3 Nephi 27:33).

Sister Elaine Dalton, who has completed many marathons, made this interesting comparison, "So it is with life. It is daily diligence with prayer and scripture study that will help you reach your goals. Your daily decisions will influence generations" (Dalton, 2003). Sister Dalton also counseled those who have gotten off course to quickly get back on:

> "If I were going the wrong way in the middle of a marathon, and I realized my mistake, would I keep going? I would immediately turn around! Why? Because I would have lost valuable time and precious energy and strength, and it would be much harder for me to finish the marathon because of this extra distance and added time. I wouldn't stay on the wrong course because no matter how long I ran there, I would never reach the finish line. And yet for many who have made a moral mistake, a little voice keeps saying: 'You blew it. You can't change. No one will ever know anyway.' To you I would say, don't believe it" (Dalton, 2009).

While sharing many similarities, spiritual marathons have some significant differences with the 26.2-mile variety. For starters, in spiritual marathons we aren't competing against anyone else. Additionally, there's hardly anything we could do to become disqualified from the race. In a profound First Presidency Message, entitled, "Finish with Your Torch Lit," President Uchtdorf taught:

> "The only way we can lose is by giving in or giving up. Sometimes after stumbling, failing, or even giving up,

we get discouraged and believe our light has gone out and our race is lost. But I testify that the Light of Christ cannot be extinguished. It shines in the darkest night and will relight our hearts if only we incline our hearts to Him" (1 Kings 8:58).

"No matter how often or how far we fall, the Light of Christ ever burns brightly. And even in the deepest night, if we but step toward Him, His light will consume the shadows and reignite our souls" (Uchtdorf, 2015).

Last of all, it doesn't really matter what pace we're running nor the stage of the race we're in - so long as we're striving to move forward. "As long as we continue to rise up and move toward our Savior, we win the race with our torches burning brightly" (Uchtdorf, 2015). The goal is making the effort to move in the right direction. Elder Renlund beautifully articulated it this way:

"No matter how long we have been off the path or how far away we have wandered, the moment we decide to change, God helps us return. From God's perspective, through sincere repentance and pressing forward with a steadfastness in Christ, once back on the path, it will be as if we were never off. The Savior pays for our sins and frees us from the looming decrease in happiness and blessings. This is referred to in the scriptures as forgiveness. After baptism, all members slip off the path—some of us even dive off. Therefore, exercising faith in Jesus Christ, repenting, receiving help from Him, and being forgiven are not onetime events but lifelong processes, processes that are repetitive and iterative. This is how we 'endure to the end'" (Renlund, 2018).

Summary

While much has been made of the importance and process of improving spiritual fitness in this book, let's keep in mind that it's not so much about *our* personal strength as it is about gaining access to *His*. He is the one who makes our "weak things strong" (Ether 12:27) and it is by His grace that "…individuals … receive strength and assistance to do good works that they otherwise would not be able to [do]… This grace is an enabling power" (Church, 2013).

Thus, becoming More Fit 4 the Kingdom isn't about comparing ourselves with others. That comparison robs us of the joy our personal progress along the path was designed to bring. Becoming More Fit 4 the Kingdom is about evaluating how we were in the past, to how we are today, to how we want to be in the future. We recognize where we are good, identify where we want to be better, and then courageously move in that direction. By applying this process throughout our lives, we qualify to say along with Paul, "I have fought a good fight, I have finished my course, I have kept the faith: Henceforth there is laid up for me a crown of righteousness, which the Lord, the righteous judge, shall give me at that day…" (2 Tim. 4:7-8).

RUN YOUR OWN RACE | *core concepts*

- All who have a willingness to repent (change and improve) and a desire to become more righteous (more spiritual fit) can find joy in the process of becoming More Fit 4 the Kingdom.

- Lindsey Jacobellis lost a gold by letting her guard down and falling in the Olympics, but she hasn't let that moment defeat or define her. She not only got back on course in that race but has continued to race to this day.

- The "race of life" isn't about "winning" in the way we traditionally think. It's about trying, failing, strategizing, strengthening, changing, improving, then trying and sometimes failing again.

- It's not so much a matter of whether we'll crash or go off course, as much as it's about whether we'll choose to continue to reach out for the Savior when we do.

- Goals and plans are essential components of race day success, but you always need to be ready to make adjustments – even some concessions – along the way.

- Part of being self-reliant is learning that we've never done all we can until we've sought help from the Lord and our loved ones. Simply put, we can't do it without them, especially Him.

- No matter how long we've been off the path or how long we've wandered, once we're back on the path it is as if we were never off.

- Becoming More Fit 4 the Kingdom is about evaluating how we were in the past, to how we are today, to how we want to be in the future. We recognize where we are good, identify where we want to be better, and then courageously move in that direction.

Appendix
"APPLICATION & DISCUSSION" QUESTIONS & WORKSHEETS

APPLICATION & DISCUSSION | INTRO | 1.0

Consider "Where You Stand" by answering the following questions:

1. *"What strategies and game plans need to be implemented?"*
    Consider the course you and your family are on. What strategies
    do you need to employ?

    - Something to start: _____
    - Something to stop: _____
    - Something to continue: _____

2. *"What difficulties lie ahead?"* What challenges do you foresee
    coming? Consider the challenging and/or tempting scenarios
    that may come your way and what plan of action you'll take
    when they do?

    _____
    _____
    _____
    _____
    _____
    _____
    _____
    _____

3. *"Am I receiving the training and spiritual fitness required?"* How
    engaged have you and your family been in spiritual fitness?
    Consider your training and involvement in fundamental
    exercises like scripture reading, prayer, church attendance, and
    others. Are you hitting the spiritual gym on a regular basis? Are
    you listening to the coaches – Prophets, Parents, Church
    Leaders?

    _____
    _____
    _____
    _____
    _____
    _____
    _____
    _____

APPLICATION & DISCUSSION | CH 1 | 1.0
Consider and share how repentance, change and improvement, has strengthened you:

1. *What is an area that you or your family have already worked at and been successful in improving?*

_____
_____
_____
_____
_____
_____
_____
_____
_____
_____

2. *How might life be different had that change not been made?*

_____
_____
_____
_____
_____
_____
_____
_____
_____
_____

APPLICATION & DISCUSSION | CH 1 |1.1

Carefully evaluate whether you or your family have accepted the *"I can't change"* or *"I shouldn't change"* philosophy in any of the four areas of fitness. Are there areas in which you've concluded, *"That's just the way I am"* or *"That's just the way we are."*

1. Wisdom – *In your intellectual fitness efforts?*

    _____
    _____
    _____
    _____
    _____

2. Stature – *In your physical fitness efforts?*

    _____
    _____
    _____
    _____
    _____

3. In Favor with God – *In your spiritual fitness efforts?*

    _____
    _____
    _____
    _____
    _____

4. In Favor with Man – *In your social fitness efforts?*

    _____
    _____
    _____
    _____
    _____

APPLICATION & DISCUSSION: CHAPTER 2 | 1.0				
The MOREFIT Goal Setting & Achieving Strategy				
Luke 2:52	1. In Writing 2. Realistic & Reported 3. Emotionally Connected 4. Measurable 5. Timely & Tied to an Action 6. Fear Confronting & Flexible 7. One Word or One Phrase-able			

WISDOM / INTELLECTUAL

1:

2:

3:

4:

5:

6:

7:

STATURE / PHYSICAL

1:

2:

3:

4:

5:

6:

7:

FAVOR WITH GOD / SPIRITUAL

1:

2:

3:

4:

5:

6:

7:

FAVOR WITH MAN / SOCIAL

1:

2:

3:

4:

5:

6:

7:

APPLICATION & DISCUSSION | CH 3 | 1.0

Evaluate your personal and family scripture study plan and consider how you can make it more effective:

1. *Am I more worried about turning pages, or turning my heart toward God?*

    _____

2. *Am I just reading, or am I taking time to ponder what I'm studying?*

    _____

3. *Am I praying for understanding before, during, or after I study?*

    _____

4. *Am I asking questions and recording questions I have?*

    _____

5. *Am I seeking revelation as part of my study?*

    _____

6. *How I plan to measure my scripture study moving forward:*

    _____

7. *What other spiritual exercises could I incorporate into my life?*

    _____
    _____
    _____
    _____
    _____
    _____
    _____
    _____

APPLICATION & DISCUSSION | CH 4 | 1.0
Answer the questions posed by Elder Bednar:

1. *Is the load I'm carrying producing the needed spiritual traction to enable me to press forward with faith in Christ on the strait and narrow path and avoid getting stuck?*

   _____

   _____

   _____

   _____

   _____

   _____

   _____

2. *Is the load I am carrying creating sufficient spiritual traction so I ultimately can return home to Heavenly Father?*

   _____

   _____

   _____

   _____

   _____

   _____

   _____

3. *How about as a family – to we have the spiritual traction needed to stick together through the challenges that lie ahead?*

   _____

   _____

   _____

   _____

   _____

   _____

   _____

APPLICATION & DISCUSSION | CH 4 | 1.1

Consider how you can "be a little more" for answering the following questions:

1. *Which of these "we can be a little more" statements resonate with you as a way you want to improve? How do you think that will be impactful in your life to do so?*

_____

_____

_____

_____

_____

_____

_____

_____

_____

_____

_____

_____

2. *What about as a family? Which "we can be a little more" statements seem to fit a family need for improvement?*

_____

_____

_____

_____

_____

_____

_____

_____

_____

_____

_____

_____

APPLICATION & DISCUSSION | CH 4 | 1.2
Consider what it means to take a "productive pause."

1. *What are some ways you've found to take a "productive pause" as you strive to progress?*

_____

_____

_____

_____

_____

_____

_____

_____

2. *What does that look like and how have you found it helpful?*

_____

_____

_____

_____

_____

_____

_____

_____

APPLICATION & DISCUSSION | CH 4 | 1.3

Consider how we try to identify areas to improve in and still remain positive:

1. *What are some truths you've learned that help identify weaknesses but not become weakened in the process?*

    _____

    _____

    _____

    _____

    _____

    _____

    _____

    _____

    _____

    _____

    _____

APPLICATION & DISCUSSION | CH 5 | 1.0

Consider how the exercises and promises above have or could impact you and your family:

1. *Identify 1-2 of the exercises above that you're already doing well:*

_____
_____
_____
_____
_____
_____
_____
_____

2. *Identify 1-2 of the exercises above you want to improve in:*

_____
_____
_____
_____
_____
_____
_____
_____

3. *Identify a promise that you most sincerely want to secure:*

_____
_____
_____
_____
_____
_____
_____
_____

THE 4 AREAS OF FITNESS	DURATION: The length of time spent doing the exercise	FREQUENCY: The number of times each week or month	INTENSITY: The level of focus or specificity
DISCUSSION & APPLICATION: CHAPTER 5 | 1.1 **Overcoming Plateaus**			
WISDOM INTELLECTUAL EXERCISE:			
STATURE PHYSICAL EXERCISE:			
FAVOR WITH GOD SPIRITUAL EXERCISE:			
FAVOR WITH MAN SOCIAL EXERCISE:			

Bibliography
MORE FIT 4 THE KINGDOM

Anderson, Spiritual Whirlwinds, General Conference, April, 2014

Ballard, Return and Receive, General Conference, April, 2007

Ballard, The Greatest Generation of Missionaries, General Conference, October, 2002

Ballard, To Whom Shall We Go, General Conference, October, 2016

Bednar, Bear Up Their Burdens with Ease, General Conference, April, 2014

Bednar, Pray Always, General Conference, October, 2008

Benson, So Shall Ye Reap, 1960, p.140

Britannica, Online Encyclopedia, updated Dec. 19, 2017

Brother Durrant, My Heart Pondereth Them Continually, General Conference, October 2015

Carroll, Alice's Adventures in Wonderland, 1898, 89.

Christofferson, The Divine Gift of Repentance, General Conference, October, 2011.

Christofferson, Why the Church, General Conference, October 2015

Church of Jesus Christ of Latter-day Saints, Children & Youth of the Church of Jesus Christ of Latter-Day Saints, An Introductory Guide for Parents and Leaders, May, 2019

Church of Jesus Christ of Latter-day Saints, For the Strength of Youth, Go Forward with Faith, 2011

Church of Jesus Christ of Latter-day Saints, Gospel Teaching and Learning Handbook, Section 2.3.1, 2012

Church of Jesus Christ of Latter-day Saints, Grace, Bible Dictionary, 2013

Church of Jesus Christ of Latter-day Saints, Marriage & Family, Doctrinal Mastery Core Document, 2016

Church of Jesus Christ of Latter-day Saints, More Holiness Give Me, Hymns, 2002

Church of Jesus Christ of Latter-day Saints, What Does the Church's New Initiative for Children and Youth Mean for You and Your Family?, Scott Taylor, lds.org, Posted May 11, 2018

Clark, Conference Report, October, 1953, p. 84

Clark, Eyes to See and Ears to Hear, General Conference, October 2015

Dalton, Press Forward and Be Steadfast, General Conference, April, 2003

Dalton, Zion is the Pure in Heart, Brigham Young University Devotional, September 13, 2009

Eden, Stroke of Madness, ESPN the Magazine: Tiger Woods Reinvents His Swing, 22 January, 2013

Eyring, An Evening with President Hinckley, 7 February 2003

Eyring, Do Not Delay, General Conference, October, 1999

Eyring, Raising Our Sights, Church Educational System, 14 Aug 2001

Eyring, The Lord Will Multiply the Harvest, Teaching Seminary: Preservice Readings 2004, 93–98

Goodgame, The Game of Risk, Time Magazine, 06 Aug 2000

Grant, Persistence, Chapter 4, Teachings of Presidents of the Church, 2011

Green, Bob. Chicago Tribune, May 15, 1991

Hallstrom, What Manner of Men, General Conference, April, 2014

Hinckley, We Have a Work to Do, General Conference, April, 1995

Hinckley, A Challenging Time—a Wonderful Time, Teaching Seminary: Preservice

Hilbig, Quench Not the Spirit Which Quickens the Inner Man, General Conference, October, 2007

Readings, Church Educational System manual, 2004

Holland, Be Ye Therefore Perfect – Eventually, General Conference, October, 2017

Holland, For Times of Trouble, Ensign, March 1980

Holland, How to Change, Liahona, February 2017

Holland, We Are All Enlisted, General Conference, October, 2011

Kaufmann, What Predicts NBA Success? Scientific American Blog Network, August 5, 2014

Kimball, The Teachings of Spencer W. Kimball, 1982, 48

Klebingat, Approaching the Throne of God with Confidence, General Conference, Apr. 2014

Lee, Stand Ye In Holy Places, Ensign, July, 1973

Maxwell, Whom the Lord Loveth, Deseret Book, 2003, 7-8

Middleton, 75 Motivational Michael Jordan Quotes, Addicted2Success.com, Jan 14, 2016

Monson, A Royal Priesthood, General Conference, October, 2007

Monson, Choices, General Conference, April, 2016

Monson, Constant Truths for Changing Times, General Conference, October, 2005

Monson, Keep the Commandments, General Conference, October, 2015

Monson, The Three R's of Choice, General Conference, October, 2010

Monson, Thou Art a Teacher Come from God, Conference Report, Oct. 1970

Moore, Historic 103-mile Swim Aided by Electric Shark Shield, cnet.com, August, 8, 2011

Myre, On Fifth Try Diana Nyad Completes Cuba-Florida Swim, npr.org, September, 2, 2013

Nelson, Hope of Israel, Worldwide Youth Devotional, June 3, 2018

Nelson, Prophets, Leadership, and Divine Law, Brigham Young University Devotional, January 8, 2017

Nelson, Revelation for the Church, Revelation for Our Lives, General Conference, April, 2018

Nelson, The Book of Mormon: What Would Your Life Be Like Without It?, General Conference, Oct. 2017

Nelson, We Can Do Better and Be Better, General Conference, April, 2019

Oaks, Good Better Best, General Conference, Oct. 2007

Oaks, Repentance and Change, General Conference, October, 2003

Pace, Crying with the Saints, Brigham Young University Devotional, Dec. 13, 1987

Packer, A Tribute to Women, Priesthood Commemoration Fireside, May 7, 1989

Packer, How to Survive in Enemy Territory, Seminary Centennial Broadcast, Jan 22, 2012

Packer, The Instrument of Your Mind and the Foundation of Your Character, CES Fireside, Feb. 2, 2003

Packer, Understanding Students, Ensign, July 1977

Renlund, Choose You This Day, General Conference, October, 2018

Robbins, Until Seventy Times Seven, General Conference, April, 2018

Roosevelt, Citizenship in a Republic, address delivered at the Sorbonne, Paris, France, 23 April 1910

Stevenson, Your Priesthood Playbook, General Conference, April, 2019

Svrluga, At the Wall, Phelps Has the Touch, Washington Post. August 16, 2008

Taylor, Why Change is So Hard and How to Make it Easier,

PsychologyToday.com, Posted October 21, 2009.

Uchtdorf, Are You Sleeping Through the Restoration, April, 2014

Uchtdorf, Finish with Your Torch Still Lit, First Presidency Message, Ensign, October 2015

Uchtdorf, Of Things That Matter Most, General Conference, October 2010

Williams, The Teachings of Harold B. Lee, 1996, 82

About the Author
SKYE FAGRELL

Skye Fagrell is married to the former Ms. Jacquelyn Sargent. They met while studying at Brigham Young University. They love each other, their family, physical fitness, and vacations that involve the ocean! Together they have four amazing children; Alexa, Makenna, Gunner, and Jayda.

Skye earned a Bachelor's degree in Visual Arts and a Minor in Coaching and Teaching Physical Education from Brigham Young University. He earned a Master's degree in Educational Leadership from Northern Arizona University. While he has advertised his willingness to exchange both degrees for a single Major League Baseball contract (preferably with the Oakland A's), he's yet to receive any takers. He still holds out hope.

Skye has worked as a professional educator and administrator for nearly 20 years, teaching seminary and institute for the Church Educational System. He's also been an online professor for Brigham Young University, Idaho. He has held many coaching and leadership positions in his community and Church. He is the CEO of *More Fit 4 Life*, where he provides life and leadership consulting and training for individuals and organizations.

More Fit 4 The Kingdom is Skye's first book. If you're interested in receiving more content similar to that outlined in this book, you can follow him on Instagram @morefit4thekingdom and @morefit4life

Made in the USA
Lexington, KY
20 December 2019